2004 POE

ONCE UPON A RHYME

IMAGINATION FOR
A NEW GENERATION

Yorkshire & Lincolnshire
Edited by Steve Twelvetree

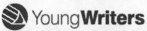 Young**Writers**

First published in Great Britain in 2004 by:
Young Writers
Remus House
Coltsfoot Drive
Peterborough
PE2 9JX
Telephone: 01733 890066
Website: www.youngwriters.co.uk

SB ISBN 1 84460 487 X

Foreword

Young Writers was established in 1991 and has been passionately devoted to the promotion of reading and writing in children and young adults ever since. The quest continues today. Young Writers remains as committed to engendering the fostering of burgeoning poetic and literary talent as ever.

This year's Young Writers competition has proven as vibrant and dynamic as ever and we are delighted to present a showcase of the best poetry from across the UK. Each poem has been carefully selected from a wealth of *Once Upon A Rhyme* entries before ultimately being published in this, our twelfth primary school poetry series.

Once again, we have been supremely impressed by the overall high quality of the entries we have received. The imagination, energy and creativity which has gone into each young writer's entry made choosing the best poems a challenging and often difficult but ultimately hugely rewarding task - the general high standard of the work submitted amply vindicating this opportunity to bring their poetry to a larger appreciative audience.

We sincerely hope you are pleased with our final selection and that you will enjoy *Once Upon A Rhyme Yorkshire & Lincolnshire* for many years to come.

Contents

Alderman Cogan's CE Primary School, Hull

Sam Goodban (10)   1
Siouxsie Bishoprick (9)   1
Paige Ostler (10)   2
Cassey McNulty (10)   2
Michael Gadd (9)   3
Dale Booth (9)   3
Bethany Thompson (9)   4
Victoria Mayne (9)   4
Bradley Rial (9)   5
John Harvey (9)   5
Jessica Fullard (9)   6
Polly Sanders (9)   6
Katie Watson (10)   7
Rebecca Brown (10)   7
Abbie Dry (9)   8
Claire Bagwell (10)   8
Robert Lane (10)   9

Bricknell Primary School, Hull

Ashley Healand (10)   9
Alice Blamires (9)   9
Calum Barnett (8)   10
Jonathan Dalby (10)   10
Chloe Underwood (8)   11
Amy Daddy (9)   11
Hannah Colthup (8)   12
Rebecca Beacock (8)   12
Kelly McRae (9)   13
Ben Lawson (10)   13

Buckingham Primary School, Hull

Joe Robinson (11)   13
Chelsea Barker (10)   14
Camron Whisby (11)   14
Katie Goodhand (10)   15
William Yorston (11)   15
Rebecca Machray (11)   16

Linzi Budgen (10)	16
James Carrick (11)	17
Ellie White (10)	17
Rebecca Shaw (11)	18

Driffield Junior School, Driffield

Charlotte Towse (11)	18
Sherrell Simmonds (11)	19
Kieron Ruse (10)	20
Georgina Lomas (11)	20
Lauren Ringrose (10)	20
Elanor Greaves (10)	21
Hannah Oxtoby (11)	21
Eve Forster (11)	22
Kirsty Longney (10)	22
Jo Ramsey (10)	23
Hollie Wilson (10)	23
Sarah Jackson (11)	24
Hollie Blakeston (10)	24
Cameron Rusbridge-Burns (11)	24
Eleanor Darlington (10)	25
Hannah Perkins (10)	25
Katy Fawcett (10)	25
Frances Dale (11)	26
Frances Wormald (10)	26
Rebecca Faulkner (10)	27
Steven Hood (11)	27
Ryan Brown (11)	27
Kate Allison (11)	28

Hornsea Primary School, Hornsea

Katie Davison (10)	29
Eleanor Fearnley (11)	29
Yvonne Weatherstone (10)	30
Millie Clarke (11)	30
Oliver Cook (10)	31
Natalie Costigan (10)	31
Grace Rollo (11)	32
Joshua Reeve (11)	32
David Knapton (10)	33
Lisa Brooke (11)	33

Harriet Taylor (10)	34
Ella Rowbotham (11)	34
Anna Railton (11)	35
Victoria Walker (11)	35
Bethany Platten (11)	36
Kayleigh Metcalfe (11)	36
Marcus Anderson (10)	37
Ailsa Williamson (10)	37
Dominic Page (10)	38
Ian Adams (11)	38
Lauren Page (10)	39
Becki Johnson (11)	39
Alice Hackney (10)	40
Molly Stephenson (11)	40
James Walker (10)	41
Joe Cox (11)	41
Glen Breary (10)	42
Ben Henderson (11)	42
Joseph Sullivan (10)	43
Jak Kershaw (10)	43
Rebecca Moir (11)	44
Danielle Davison (10)	44
Hannah Watson (11)	45
Michael McNeil (10)	45
Sean Howcroft (10)	46
Andrew Barr (11)	46
Jade McKenzie (10)	47
Stuart Green (10)	47
Charlotte Ridley (11)	48
Ben Cooper (11)	48
Annie Hilton (10)	49
Jamie Wright (12)	50
Joe Williams (10)	50
Taylor Giles (11)	51
Matthew Roberts (10)	51
Lucy Wallwork (10)	52
Ashleigh Robinson (11)	53
Hannah Rawson (10)	53
Kevin Button (10)	54
Joseph Singleton (10)	54
Mollie Thompson (11)	55
Sam Hayden (10)	55

Kingsway Primary School, Goole

Lauren Deakin (11)	56
Christopher Masterman (10)	57
Rebecca Quarmby (10)	57
Megan Garland (10)	58
Luke Patchett (10)	59
Dallas Woods (10)	60
Adam Hairsine (10)	60
James Sharpe (10)	61

Kirmington CE Primary School, Kirmington

Thomas Ansell (11)	61
Lauren Roberts (9)	61
Lillie Laverick (9)	62
Nicholas Cassidy (11)	62
Chloe Rear (9)	62
Aaron Woods (8)	63
Joanne Watson (9)	63
Sam Thompson (10)	63
Shannon Bailey (9)	64

Longhill Primary School, Hull

Megan Bell (8)	64
Yasmin Cox	64
Danny Grayson (8)	65
Naomi McLaren	65
Darian Francis	65
Brendon Scott	65
Rebecca Casey (8)	66
Liam Rudd (10)	66
Mathew Headon (8)	66
Claire Sanderson (10)	67
Christopher Wheeldon (10)	67
Christopher Strafford (7)	68

Newington Primary School, Hull

Kye Smith (8)	68
Abigail Bonehill (9)	68
Sophie Greene (9)	69
Leah Cochran (7)	69
Daniel Taylor (8)	69

Naomi Hassan (9)	70
Mirza Ibrisimovic (9)	70
Anthony Arnott (9)	70
Keiran Scholey (10)	71
Chelsea Clark (8)	71
Alexander Wilson (8)	72

Old Clee Junior School, Grimsby

Katie Higham (11)	72
Amy Hopkinson (10)	72
Amy Kearns (11)	73
Drew Morgan (9)	73
Daniel Stuffin (7)	74
Daniel Chesman (8)	74
Emma Butler (10)	75
Bethany Roberts (9)	75
Tom Taylor (9)	76
Lucy Webb (11)	76
Hannah Stuffin (9)	77
Dawn Spurrell (9)	77
Shelby Fountain (9)	78
Joshua Chester (9)	78
Hollie Barber (10)	79
Fay Sewell (10)	79
Alex Revell (11)	80
Hannah Wright (10)	80
Jessica Salkeld (11)	81
Charlotte Pleasants (9)	81
Harriet Dales (10)	82
Grant Zeebroek (9)	83
Lewis Watson (9)	83
Amy Coleman (8)	83
Claire Croft (11)	84
Josh Barley (8)	84
Lewis Patterson (10)	84
Kerrigan Brown (9)	85
Callum Vick (9)	85
Keane Boothby (10)	86
Paul Cole (9)	86
Bethany Webb (9)	87
Sophie Lewis (7)	87

Jessica Norfolk (7)   88
Elizabeth Summers (9)   88
Sophie Dolan (10)   89
Khloe-Celia Jennings (10)   89
Teresa Shortland (10)   90
Jessica Wortley (8)   90

Pasture Primary School, Goole
Sam Phillipson (9)   90
Daniel Graves (10)   91
Joshua Oldridge (9)   91
Sophie Lloyd (7)   92
Alice Shipley (9)   92
Samuel Duffin (9)   93
Abbie Butler (8)   93
Sophie Harrison (11)   94
Grant Bellis (9)   94
Matthew Fenwick (11)   95
Matthew Harrison (10)   96
Bethany Wraith (9)   96
Johnathan Ross-Paterson (11)   97
Liam Watson (10)   97
Melissa Leyland (8)   98
Luke Kendall (9)   98
Thomas Lambert (8)   99
Jack Sowerby (10)   99
Adam Scott (9)   100
Tanya Boyce (10)   100
Rebecca Naylor (11)   101
Jemma Brown (10)   102
Amy Nicholls (10)   103
Morgan Linnington (9)   103
Charlotte Kenning (10)   104
Rhys Siddons (9)   104
Jade Batty (10)   105
Rhys James (10)   105
Rebecca Hardman (10)   106
Matthew Graves (9)   106
Holly Wilkinson (9)   107
Monica Ip (10)   107
Jake Lewis (9)   108

Priory Primary School, Hull
Jamie Chilcott (10)   108

Snaith CP School, Snaith
Jasmine Wright (10)   109
Katie Oliver (10)   109
Heather King (9)   110
Jessica Holmes (10)   110
Rebecca Watts (10)   111
Georgina Gallagher (10)   111

Sutton Park Primary School, Kingston-upon-Hull
Amy Brice (8)   112
Shannon Carr (10)   112
Emma Smith (8)   113
James Mobbs (9)   113
Bethany Watson (9)   114
Sarah Sharpless (10)   114
Ian Parr (9)   115
Jeff Humphrey (10)   116
Amy Mumby (8)   116
Laura Andrew (8)   117
Lauren Spenceley (8)   117
Ashley Edmonds (9)   118
Kieron Wegg (8)   118
Kerry Baxter (7)   119
James Piercy (7)   119
Adam Herbert (7)   119
Emily Sparne (9)   120
Laura Jackson (7)   120
Claire Hambly (7)   120
Ria Richardson (7)   121
Danielle Bellamy (7)   121
Patrick Langdale (7)   121
Amy Aistrop (9)   122
James Pinder (8)   122
Jasmin Russell (7)   122
Joshua Ffoulkes (8)   123
Justin Phillips (7)   123
Sophie Edwards (8)   123

Paige Denton (11)   124
Chelsey Dixon (8)   124
Caleb Higgins (9)   125
Liam Senior (9)   125
Luke Watkinson (8)   125
Charlotte Morgan (10)   126
Dale Dermott, Christopher Harding, Michael Seaman, Aiden
    Tidswell, Steven Bolton, & Ashley Hatton-Brown (9)   126
Dale Hickingbotham (9)   127

Thorpepark Primary School, Hull

Adam Green (10)   127
Ryan Westerdale-Price & Natasha Harding (10)   128
Casey Watson (10)   128
Aaron Simpson (9)   129
Rebecca Turton (9)   129
Carl Robinson (10)   130
Jessica Rayner (10)   130
David Harrison (10)   131
Amanda Marquis (10)   131
Rebecca Lang (9)   132
Michael Stark (10)   132
Ryan Malton (10)   133
Kelsea Scoins (9)   133
Demi Hodgins (10)   134
Daniel Jones (9)   135
Nathan Schofield (10)   135
Nicola Pilkington (10)   136
Kade Cooke (9)   136
Tammy Milner & Charlotte Rowan (10)   137
Kristina Green (9)   137
Bradley Franklin (9)   138
Jamie Nolan (9)   138
Laura Chaffer (9)   139
Georgina Drewery (9)   139
Sarah Mellors (10)   140
Ashley Fox (9)   140
Jarrod Nicholson (10)   141
Tony Clark (9)   141
David Benford (10)   141

Josh Nichols (9)	142
Ryan Thomas (9)	142
Nicky Robinson (10)	142

Tilbury Primary School, Hull

Jack Humphries (9)	143
Jake Jones (9)	144
Ellie Dale (9)	144
Robbie Gillyon (9)	144
Joshua Beavers (10)	145
Laura Smith (9)	145
Amber Humphries (10)	146
Callum Stone (9)	146
Danielle Sowersby (10)	147
David Benn (10)	147
Vincent Brooks (10)	148
Andrew Benn (10)	148
Ryan Lawler (10)	149
Abigail Ellis (9)	150
Christina Smith (10)	150
Jasmine Chilvers (9)	151
Sophie Langley (10)	151
Jarrad Grainger (9)	152
Shannen Smith (9)	152
Jack Sullivan (9)	153
Liam Sawyers (9)	153
Sean Kemp (9)	154
Chelsea West (9)	154
Chantelle Dixon (10)	155
Louis Burdett (10)	155

Withernwick Primary School, Hull

Katy Simpson (10)	156
Heather Croft (8)	156
William Rowley (11)	157
Zoe Mitchell (10)	157
Daniel Walker (9)	158

Wold Primary School, Hull

| Craig Pitts (10) | 158 |
| Amy Kerman (11) | 159 |

Louis Cook (9)   159
Gareth Mathie (8)   160
Tessa Grimes (10)   160
Stephen Forton (10)   161
Ashley Hill (10)   161
Nikki Brown (9)   162
Stephanie Kinch (9)   162
Jordan Eastwood (9)   163
Bethany Lowden (9)   163
Hannah Bromby (8)   164
Laura Cawthra (9)   165
Lauren McNeil (9)   165
Reece Harvey (8)   166
Sammie-Jay Hackett (9)   166
Gemma Iveson (8)   167
Darcey Black-Foy   168
Sam Baker (10)   169
Jenna Stewart (10)   169
Richard Clayphan (9)   170
Jamie Mosey (9)   170
Joe Marshall (10)   171
Emma Farnill (9)   171
Natasha Taylor (7)   172
Ryan Stothard (7)   172
Abigail Hastings (8)   173
Eden Scott Brown (7)   173
Stacy Peacham (7)   174
Jamie King (10)   174
Calum Thompson (8)   175
Emma Haywood (9)   176
Luke Wilkinson (9)   176
Jennifer Hewson (8)   177
Amy Kemp (8)   178
Jessica Harris (8)   179
Wesley Foster (8)   180
Victoria Marshall (8)   181
Tim Sainty (8)   182
Naomi Mason (8)   183
Eve Morton (8)   184
Jack Walsh (8)   185
Harry John Foster (8)   186
Amy Twidale (10)   186

Jason Carey (8)	187
Emmie Foster (9)	187
Chloé Hayzelden (8)	188
Catherine Welham (8)	189
Joe Morris (8)	190
Megan Hackford (9)	191
Ricky Hookem (10)	191
Jack Laverick (10)	191
Gareth Hales (10)	192
Chelsea Shepherd (10)	192
Adam Owston-Dale (10)	193
Joshua Rae (9)	193
Ryan Gagg (8)	194
Alexander Powell (9)	194

The Poems

Hate And Love

Hate is black
Like volcanic ash
It lives somewhere inside you
It sounds like a thunderstorm
Loud and scary
It tastes like chilli pepper
So hot and spicy
It feels painful
Like you've been hit in the stomach
Hate is horrible.

Love is pink and red
Like rose on Valentine's
It lives deep, deep down inside you
It sounds like a love song
Beautiful and quiet
It tastes like chicken pie
So nice and warm
It feels like someone has hugged you
Nice feeling
Love is like a soft cushion.

Sam Goodban (10)
Alderman Cogan's CE Primary School, Hull

Hate

Hate is the colour of a dull black house
It smells like burnt toast
But it tastes like hot pepper.

Hate sounds like a thunderbolt flying in the air
It feels like a burnt roof lying on the floor
But it looks like burning fire just standing.

Siouxsie Bishoprick (9)
Alderman Cogan's CE Primary School, Hull

Love And Hate

Love is a beautiful rainbow
It smells like a field of poppies
Sounds exciting just like you
It makes you feel a warm glow
It lives in your heart and in the air
And all around
And that is love.

Hate is a dull rusty black colour
It smells like a burnt out car
The sound gives you a booming headache
It lives like an old box
And that is hate
You won't like that.

Paige Ostler (10)
Alderman Cogan's CE Primary School, Hull

Aliens On Mars

Aliens come from Mars
They don't drive cars
They look like little bushes
They don't drive buses
They have blue and white veins
They don't drive trains
They live on the moon
They don't eat with a spoon
They travel around in spaceships
They don't eat *chips!*

Cassey McNulty (10)
Alderman Cogan's CE Primary School, Hull

Power And Weakness

Power is jet black
Power smells as sweet as you want
It tastes like blood
It's the sound of the devil
It feels like molten rock scolding your hand
It lives in the fires of hell
Power waits for nobody.

Weakness is a blank piece of white paper
It smells like flaming petrol
It tastes like a bitter-sweet cup of tea
It sounds like a TV with no aerial
It feels like the feather of a dove
Weakness lives in the middle of your mind
Weakness waits for everybody.

Michael Gadd (9)
Alderman Cogan's CE Primary School, Hull

Love

Love is red
Like a love heart
It smells wonderful
Like my mother's perfume
It sounds like butterfly wings flapping in the wind
It feels soft like a cushion
It tastes like honey so sweet
It lives in the heart forever.

Dale Booth (9)
Alderman Cogan's CE Primary School, Hull

Love And Hate

Love is the colour of peach.
Love smells like strawberries
Love looks like a field of poppies
It sounds like robins singing
Love tastes like freshly cooked chocolate
Melting in a pan
Love lives in your heart.

Hate is the colour black just like the night sky
Hate smells like toxic fumes
It looks like a rubbish dump where everyone puts their rubbish
Hate smells like gone off cheese that's gone mouldy overnight
Hate tastes like custard and beans mixed up together
Hate lives in an erupting volcano.

Bethany Thompson (9)
Alderman Cogan's CE Primary School, Hull

Love And Hate

Love is the colour of all the bright colours in the rainbow
It smells like a summer morning
It tastes like ice cream
Love sounds like whistling birds
Love feels great and beautiful
Love lives inside me.

Hate is the colour of black and grey
It smells like war in the winter
It tastes dull
Hate sounds like fighting and screaming
It lives inside everyone.

Victoria Mayne (9)
Alderman Cogan's CE Primary School, Hull

Peace And War

Peace is a light green colour, like the morning fields,
It tastes like the scent of a flower,
It tastes like chocolate straight from the freezer,
It sounds like a gentle breeze in the distance,
It feels like everything is wonderful inside you,
It lives in a great castle on the hill.

War is grey and dull, like a wet day when the sun isn't out,
It smells like burning gas
It tastes like sprouts for your Sunday roast
It sounds like guns and bombs from a distant land
It feels like everything is horrible inside
It lives in a dark and gloomy hut
Peace is better than war.

Bradley Rial (9)
Alderman Cogan's CE Primary School, Hull

Love And Hate

Love is the colour of peace and flowers,
It's the smell of lilac and vanilla
It tastes of apples and orange,
Love is the sound of the trees rustling in the wind,
Love feels soft and rich,
It lives in your heart so keep it safe,
Hate is the colour of black and grey,
It's the smell of allies and fumes,
It tastes of horrible sprouts,
Hate is the sound of explosions and car engines,
Hate is the feel of pain and cruelty
It lives in darkness so keep it away.

John Harvey (9)
Alderman Cogan's CE Primary School, Hull

Love

Love is the colour of red
Like poppies growing on a fresh field.

Love tastes like ice cream with chocolate sauce on top
On a hot summer's day.

Love smells like flowers
And fresh green grass on a flower field.

Love sounds like birds chirping
In the tall green trees.

Love feels like a warm piece of heart
For someone or something special.

Love lives in your body inside the heart.

Jessica Fullard (9)
Alderman Cogan's CE Primary School, Hull

Hate And Love

Hate is the colour of dark grey
In the cloudy, windy sky,
Hate is the sound of base drums,
Making people cry.

Love is the colour of lilac
It is the sound of musical notes,
It is a journey through the quiet land of dreams
On a wonderful, dreaming boat.

Polly Sanders (9)
Alderman Cogan's CE Primary School, Hull

Love And Hate

Love is every colour like glitter falling from the sky,
It smells like freshly cut flowers,
It tastes like the world's best ice cream,
It sounds like a slow piece of music with a beautiful beat,
It feels like the wind gently blowing against me,
It lives everywhere in your heart.

Hate is the colour black,
It smells burnt,
It tastes like a burnt piece of toast,
It sounds like a war,
It feels like a lightning bolt hitting you,
It lives all over the world.

Katie Watson (10)
Alderman Cogan's CE Primary School, Hull

Love And Hate

Love is rosy red
Hate is dark purple
Love smells like someone giving you flowers.
Hate smells like someone who's been sick
Love tastes like every bit of food in the world
Hate tastes like hot lava running out of a volcano
Love sounds like the tune of love
Hate sounds like people being horrible to you
Love feels like you've got all the time in the world
Hate feels like you've got no space in the world
Love lives in your heart
Hate lives in your brain.

Rebecca Brown (10)
Alderman Cogan's CE Primary School, Hull

Hate And Love

Hate is black as the midnight dark
It smells like old milk left in the sun too long
It sounds like a broken record player
It tastes like rotten sprouts
It feels like a big solid rock
It lives somewhere inside
You
Love is as red as a rose
It is something sweet
It tastes like chocolate on a spring day
It sounds like a harp playing softly and sweetly
It feels like something soft and bubbly
It lives inside your heart.

Abbie Dry (9)
Alderman Cogan's CE Primary School, Hull

Anger And Love

Anger is black behind a door never opened
Lava spreading all over
Ashes burnt with a taste of heart
Screams of pain to kill the world
Been stabbed a thousand times with nobody to help you
Deep inside my heart.

A burgundy red next to a warm fire burning
The smell of roses through a field with grass and corn growing
Fresh strawberries just picked with clotted cream all over them
Trees rustling with twigs and leaves crunching
You are there forever and can't escape and have it forever
It lives deep inside somewhere.

Claire Bagwell (10)
Alderman Cogan's CE Primary School, Hull

Love

Love is sweet and also savoury
A flower will last for hours and hours.
It smells like a fresh smell of summer.
Hate is black
Just like a dust sack
The taste for me is slime
And I can hear the sound of a sign.

Robert Lane (10)
Alderman Cogan's CE Primary School, Hull

Death

Death is dark and black,
Death tastes like mud,
It smells of blood,
It sounds like a pencil snapping,
It feels like hearts breaking,
Death lives underground.

Ashley Healand (10)
Bricknell Primary School, Hull

Disease

Disease is Marilyn Manson black,
It smells like foul medicine,
Disease tastes of sour lemons,
It sounds like roaring screams,
It feels like being stabbed,
Disease lives in an old poison jar.

Alice Blamires (9)
Bricknell Primary School, Hull

As, As, As

As fat as a pig,
As curly as a wig,
As hot as a fire,
As cold as a liar,
As sharp as teeth,
As weak as a leaf,
As runny as honey,
As shiny as money,
As soft as a bunny,
As fat as a tummy,
As hot as an iron,
As fierce as a lion,
As chilly as ice,
As yummy as rice,
As fast as a car,
As small as a jar,
As tall as a wall,
As funny as a troll,
As big as a clue,
As nice as *you!*

Calum Barnett (8)
Bricknell Primary School, Hull

Hope

Hope is the colour of a canary
It smells like flowers in the field
Hope tastes of chocolate cake
It sounds like a choir singing
It feels like a pillow
Hope lives in your heart.

Jonathan Dalby (10)
Bricknell Primary School, Hull

As, As, As

As slow as snow,
As warm as a glow,
As fast as a car,
As black as tar,
As hot as fudge,
As grimy as sludge,
As disgusting as a worm,
As frizzy as a perm,
As mucky as a pig,
As stupid as a wig,
As wobbly as a tooth,
As good as the truth,
As sharp as razors,
As cool as blazers,
As fierce as a dog,
As steamy as fog.

Chloe Underwood (8)
Bricknell Primary School, Hull

Hate

Hate is putrid purple
It smells like boiled eggs
Hate tastes of sea salt,
It sounds like screaming
It feels spiky
Hate lives in a bonfire.

Amy Daddy (9)
Bricknell Primary School, Hull

The Haunted House

In the cellar . . .
Creaking shutters slamming in the wind,
Creepy spiders waltzing in a tin,
Abandoned, soleless shoe thrown under the bed,
Tarnished candlestick rolling around the floor,
In the haunted house.

In the attic . . .
Squeaking bats gliding all around
Forgotten photos stored up high
Rotting brown paper scattered on the floor,
In the haunted house.

In the bedroom . . .
Faded China doll slumped in a corner,
Battered slipper hidden under the bed.
Voices from memory trickling round my head,
In the haunted house.

Hannah Colthup (8)
Bricknell Primary School, Hull

Inside The Ice Arena

Inside the ice arena, cold and wet
Inside the locker, dark and dusty
Inside the sled, warm and comfy
Inside the skates, scrunched.
Inside the car, small and warm.
Inside the seat, warm, comfy and soft.
Inside the house, lovely and warm.

Rebecca Beacock (8)
Bricknell Primary School, Hull

Poison

Inside the cobra's fang, the sandy desert.
Inside the sandy desert, the cobra's coils.
Inside the cobra's coils, the fresh oasis.
Inside the fresh oasis, the cobra's scales.
Inside the cobra's scales, the pyramid.
Inside the pyramid, the cobra's fang.

Kelly McRae (9)
Bricknell Primary School, Hull

Death

Death is pitch-black,
It smells like a burnt out candle,
Death tastes like poison,
It sounds like a scream, a thud,
It feels like a stabbing pain,
Death lives in a coffin.

Ben Lawson (10)
Bricknell Primary School, Hull

Homework

I have to write a poem
I ask my mum for some help
But she said no because I had to write it myself.
So I watch a bit of telly,
Then I ask my dad for some help.
But he was in his own world.
I have an idea to go to school without my poem.

Joe Robinson (11)
Buckingham Primary School, Hull

My Dog Sugar

My dog Sugar is brown and grey.
She is not scared of anyone.
She always fights me with me and my brother.

At night she always comes in my bed.
She sometimes chews my quilt.
So I have lots of holes.

She always runs about.
Sometimes even falls.
She is always on the windowsill.
When she sees us coming she gets excited.
She sometimes falls but gets back up.
She never hurts herself.

Chelsea Barker (10)
Buckingham Primary School, Hull

Footy Is The Game

Football, football is our game,
It gives you money it brings you fame.
If we win, we chant and sing,
'Cos David Beckham is footy king.

Offside, red card, free kicks,
Sometimes the referee can take the mick,
Arsenal, Liverpool and Man U.
Sunderland, Tottenham, Everton too.

They're all good teams but not the best,
'Cos Man United beat the rest.

Camron Whisby (11)
Buckingham Primary School, Hull

All About Winter

The mornings are dark
The trees are bare
Can it be winter
Out there?

The icy conditions,
The cold, cold snap
Makes me want to
Have a long, long nap.

We are looking
Forward to spring
When the leaves
Are beginning to
Come back.

Birds are singing
The days are getting lighter
Ever so brighter
I think
Nature is so
Beautiful.

Katie Goodhand (10)
Buckingham Primary School, Hull

I Want A Dog

A dog is all I want
Someone who is on my side
He'll listen to my troubles
Who will never tell my secrets?
Never ever judge me
But the answer is always *No!*
Whenever I ask for a dog the answer is *No!*
I *just* want a pet, a friend, who loves me all the time.

William Yorston (11)
Buckingham Primary School, Hull

Seasons

Spring there's lots of new things.
Bulbs in the garden start to show.
Blossom on trees start to grow.
Birds singing in the trees.
Easter is here the bunny might come
With chocolate eggs for everyone.

Nice and warm in the sun
Lots of cold drinks to keep us cool.
Go on holidays, lots of fun,
Play in the garden for more fun.
The flowers start to come.

Leaves fall off the trees,
Blown by the wind across the fields.
It's fun to play in the leaves,
It's damp and cold to make me sneeze.

It's fun to play in the snow
Time to get warm
Christmas is here
Will Santa show?
To bring toys to all good girls and boys.

Rebecca Machray (11)
Buckingham Primary School, Hull

In The Water

The crab in the sea walking on the sand
So slow
So slow.
The fish in the sea swims in the water
Really fast
Really fast.
The octopus well, I can't say much about him
He's slow and fast,
You can never tell what mood he's in!

Linzi Budgen (10)
Buckingham Primary School, Hull

Rugby

Rugby is the game where
you get broken legs and arms.

Come down and play the game
if you can handle the knocks.
If you think you're tough
come and play the rough game.

If you want lots of money
and have a smart car
come on down
join the team
if you want all that to be yours.

James Carrick (11)
Buckingham Primary School, Hull

My Budgie Roly

I have a pet called Roly,
Who chirps all the time,
Is quite greedy
But not very shy.

He runs about in his cage,
Flies around and around.
He loves to stand on my finger
And nibble at my ear
That makes me giggle all the time!

Ellie White (10)
Buckingham Primary School, Hull

Hamsters

It's night-time again
And I'm coming out to play,
Spinning in my squeaky wheel
But never during the day.

I like the noise it makes
It drives my owners mad,
But they treat me so nicely, that
I'm never bad.

I don't nibble their toes or
Bite their feet
But sometimes I wee on
Their three piece suite.

It's fun being a hamster!

Rebecca Shaw (11)
Buckingham Primary School, Hull

The Nextdoor Butler

Just because he is tall and thin,
With a big nose, that sticks right out in front of him
Doesn't mean he's mean and sly,
To be honest, he's very kind.

Like yesterday he came to play,
He did the same today,
We played for hours and hours,
Until his boss came back.

When it came to my birthday, I invited him to tea,
He brought me a lovely doll,
With golden hair and sparkling teeth,
By the end of the day we were full and tired.

What a wonderful day that had been!

Charlotte Towse (11)
Driffield Junior School, Driffield

Dream Tiger

I saw a tiger in my dream last night,
His eyes flashed yellow burning bright.
I watched from behind a leafy bush,
Fixed to the spot and very hush, hush.
He broke through the trees and stood
with a gaze,
Towards my place of hiding, I trembled in a
daze.
He was powerful and lean with huge pads
for paws,
While I am slight, but like him on all fours.

I saw a tiger in my dream last night,
But to my surprise he asked if I was alright!
'You look out of sorts on all fours like that,
A man cub trying to look like a cat.'
'From where do you come, my little friend cub?'
'I don't know,' said I, with one hand on my head
I gave a rub.
He yawned and shook his great head,
'Why you're still at home in your bed.'

I saw a tiger in my dream last night,
He was a friendly big cat to my delight.
'How do you know from where I come?' said I,
'Because many of your type visit this land in the sky.'
Together we sat and talked for a while
Till morning came I woke with a smile.
I saw a tiger in my dream last night,
No more nightmares to give me a fright.

Sherrell Simmonds (11)
Driffield Junior School, Driffield

Snow

Children playing in the snow,
Running all around.
Snowball fights everywhere,
People having fun.
Everywhere you look,
Snowmen all over.
Everyone is having
Fun today because
School is closed
It's a snow day!

Kieron Ruse (10)
Driffield Junior School, Driffield

Human Munchers

Sharp teeth,
Can't speak,
Deadly killer,
Silent swimmer,
Colour grey,
Causes dismay,
Meat crunchers,
Human munchers.

Georgina Lomas (11)
Driffield Junior School, Driffield

Pony - Haikus

Eating all the grass
Galloping through the green fields
Trotting over poles.

Going for a ride
Along a bridle pathway
Clip-clip-clip-clip-clip.

Lauren Ringrose (10)
Driffield Junior School, Driffield

War With Terrorism

Leaders want to fight,
Their goodwill in sight
How do they sleep at night?

What about the others?
What about our brothers?

In Iraq families are losing
While ours are out boozing.
Missiles firing, missiles *blazing*
While we're gazing.

Bush and Blair
Are they fair?
Do they care?

If this is war,
Who is it for?

Elanor Greaves (10)
Driffield Junior School, Driffield

Through A Winter Window

As I look
it's a frozen blanket
glistening on the world.
With nothing to disturb it,
except the frozen rain.
Snow falling silently,
gently on the icy grass,
turning into crystal shapes,
or moulded into balls.
Beautiful but cold,
Icy yet an artist,
Snow glistening on the world.

Hannah Oxtoby (11)
Driffield Junior School, Driffield

The Big Purple Monster

The big *purple* monster comes awake at night
He comes alive with a *crash and a boom*
His big purple fur covers his face
And a short stubby tail from behind.

The big *purple* monster comes awake at night
He appears in a *flash* of light
His tall thin body towers over my bed
And he whispers in my ear.

'I am the big *purple* monster
I come awake at night
The *crashes* and the *booms* and the *flashes* of the light
Are the magic of the night.'

Eve Forster (11)
Driffield Junior School, Driffield

Sam The Pig

Sam the pig lives in a sty,
He lies around under the blue sky.
His farmyard friends see him daily,
And they all know he's so lazy,
The farmer's wife brings him food,
If she's late he's in such a mood!
He stomps and charges up and down,
His mood in fact is quite profound.
One day the farmer's wife forgot him,
And oh Sam made such a din,
He charged at her and sent her flying,
Sam looked at her as she laid covered in dirt,
And realised he'd been such a jerk!

Kirsty Longney (10)
Driffield Junior School, Driffield

A Graveyard At Night

A graveyard at night,
Spooky, silent, still, scary,
Be careful someone's
Out there.

A graveyard at night,
Trees moving, wind howling,
Bushes shuffling.

A graveyard at night,
Weird forces at work,
A cat is miaowing
Or is it?

A graveyard at night,
Skeletons coming out of graves,
Ghosts appearing,
Dogs barking,
    Help!

Jo Ramsey (10)
Driffield Junior School, Driffield

ABC

ABC
Can you help me?
I don't know the rest,
Alphabet's not the best!

What's the answer to 2 x 2?
Tell me quickly, do please do!
Please, please tell me quickly,
All multiplication is sickly!

What's the square root of 4?
Maths + maths = bore, bore, bore!
Will playtime ever come?
I'm not doing the next sum!

Hollie Wilson (10)
Driffield Junior School, Driffield

Happy Hopper!

Bushy tail
Floppy ears
House burrow
Green grass
Fast runner
Carrot cruncher
Lettuce muncher.
Happy hopper!

Sarah Jackson (11)
Driffield Junior School, Driffield

Riding For Fame

Over the hurdles
Off they go
Galloping fast
As they go
Over the line
Won the race
See you soon
At the steeplechase.

Hollie Blakeston (10)
Driffield Junior School, Driffield

Darkness

Darkness,
Creeping slowly,
Covering everything,
Blinding coldness and blackness scary,
Darkness.

Cameron Rusbridge-Burns (11)
Driffield Junior School, Driffield

Petal Passion

Come in spring
Bloom in summer
Die in autumn
Different colours
All shapes and sizes
Sweet smells
Spiky stalks
Live in the ground.

Eleanor Darlington   (10)
Driffield Junior School, Driffield

Clouds

Clouds moving in the sky,
Weaving in and out of the sun,
And twisting in all shapes and sizes.

Fluffy and white
Soft as candyfloss.

Just waiting for the aeroplanes to weave in and out.
Clouds moving in the sky.

Hannah Perkins   (10)
Driffield Junior School, Driffield

Tail Bobber

Carrot muncher
Cabbage nibbler
Tail bobber
Good jumper
High hopper
Big bouncer
Cute looker.

Katy Fawcett   (10)
Driffield Junior School, Driffield

Tigers

Tigers eat a lot of food,
Pouncing for its prey,
Sometimes they get in a mood,
So don't get in their way.

Tigers have a lot of stripes
They sometimes have some fun,
Tigers come in different types,
So run, run, run.

Tigers can run really fast,
Prancing all around,
Sometimes they can even blast,
Food that they have found.

Tigers have very small ears,
And little tiny eyes,
You will never see any tears,
Sneaks up on you, surprise!

Frances Dale (11)
Driffield Junior School, Driffield

The Camel's Hump

A camel has a hump,
In the middle of its back,
An elephant hasn't,
Nor has a yak.

A tiger is stripy,
A cheetah has spots,
A centipede has legs,
Lots, lots, lots.

A fish has a fin,
A panther is all black,
But a camel has a hump,
In the middle of its back.

Frances Wormald (10)
Driffield Junior School, Driffield

Ship Sinker Kenning

Moby Dick
Come quick
Neptune's home
Has blown
Wave warrior
Brave carrier
Water drinker
Ship sinker
Boat basher
Cliff clasher
Dirt dragger
Stone stagger
Fish finder
Big minder
Water drinker
Ship sinker.

Rebecca Faulkner (10)
Driffield Junior School, Driffield

Monkeys Cinquain

Monkeys
Dancing on leaves
Swinging from tree to tree
Have you heard the monkeys screaming
Hee-hee.

Steven Hood (11)
Driffield Junior School, Driffield

January - Haikus

January snow
Melting in the New Year sun
Shrinking white snowmen.

Ryan Brown (11)
Driffield Junior School, Driffield

War

What is war?
Death is war!
Death for the world,
That is war.

Fear every day,
Fear from the bombs that come our way,
The earth rumbles
As the world crumbles.

What is war?
Death is war!
Death for the world
That is war.

Out on the battlefields,
The fighter never yields.
Running to defend,
Broken hearts never mend.

What is war?
Death is war!
Death for the world
That is war.

People falling,
Men calling,
Weapons are the worst,
They should be cursed.

What is war?
Death is war!
Death for the world,
That is war.

Many people die in war,
Why isn't it against the law?

Kate Allison (11)
Driffield Junior School, Driffield

The Storm

Bashing, crashing, flashing,
Like a torch lighting up the town,
The air swirling around.
The clouds crashing together in the gloomy grey sky.
Water falling, hitting the ground.
People can't sleep because of the awful sound.
It crashes down the door
Enters the room and whips up furniture
In a furious attack.
Shatters glass, whips round curtains,
Whirls, shakes and bashes
Every frozen object,
Slowly, calms to a gentle breeze
Quietly disappears.

Katie Davison (10)
Hornsea Primary School, Hornsea

The Storm

Crashing, colliding,
Yellow streaks, enormous whip
Bellowing loudly, crying in the wind.
Yellow streaks sharp as a knife
Travelling bravely to the ground.
A horrifying shriek from behind.
Slowly, slowly changing softly
Snow started to drip
Drips danced gracefully like a bird
Hardly laying down its feathery body.
But still carries on, never changing,
Crashing, colliding.

Eleanor Fearnley (11)
Hornsea Primary School, Hornsea

I Don't Want To Go To School Mum

'I don't want to go to school Mum,'
I said as the light flooded in the room,
The teachers are aliens
They'll lead us to our doom.

'I don't want to go to school Mum,
I'm feeling very ill.
I've got a deadly virus
And you can't cure it with a pill.'

'I don't want to go to school Mum
Oh it causes me pain,
My arms are always hurting
And my ears are aching again.'

'That's alright my dear
You don't have to go to school today'
Said Mum with a smile on her face
'Because it is a Saturday.'

Yvonne Weatherstone (10)
Hornsea Primary School, Hornsea

War

Why are people filled with hatred?
Anger explodes as people flee
Screams, shouts, crying,
The air is filled with dust,
The air is filled with stench.

Consumed with hatred
As people lay injured or dying.
Racing, rushing in panic
To escape the death and destruction.

Why are people filled with hatred?

Millie Clarke (11)
Hornsea Primary School, Hornsea

The Tornado

Total destruction, nothing stands in its way.
Spinning, destroying everything
Rushing, rushing,
Past haunted faces.
Like a black hole, sucking out life of
Everything in sight.
Smell of death and blood lie heavily in the air
And then it stops, like nothing ever
Happened . . .
Silence, calm,
Total destruction
Complete.

Oliver Cook (10)
Hornsea Primary School, Hornsea

Dolphin

Gracefully slicing through
A sea still as glass
Rippling, trickling . . .
Delicate patterns emerge
As the creature flows on.

Fins of blue - grey
Appear like a roller coaster.
Glistening eyes, darting fins,
Shattering with excitement,
Squealing with pleasure.

Gracefully slicing through . . .

Natalie Costigan (10)
Hornsea Primary School, Hornsea

Rain

Stamping the heartless grey stone.
Trickling the shivering plastic.
Rushing, racing, until it explodes.
Thunders, hurtles across the sky.
Spits on the footpaths like fireworks,
Bites at your face,
Gurgles, gushes, glistens.
The golden yolk sun rises,
Wondrous light cloaks each drop,
Starting to stamp, trickle, rush, race again.
Thunders hurtles across the sky,
Spits on the footpaths like fireworks,
Bites at your face,
Gurgles, gushes, glistens.

Grace Rollo (11)
Hornsea Primary School, Hornsea

Sun

Swirling, burning, beaming, scorching.
A yellow furnace moving slowly.
Stretching its arms across the universe,
Rising in a setting beyond the horizon,
Whispering silently as it soars.

Darker, deeper hides its feelings,
A multitude of luxurious colours,
Pinks, oranges, buttercup yellows,
Beautifully expressing its vibrant purpose.

Swirling, burning, beaming, scorching,
Ensure life on Earth.

Joshua Reeve (11)
Hornsea Primary School, Hornsea

Escape

Run, run like the wind,
Footsteps pounding behind.
Shadows creeping closer and closer,
Panic, heart racing,
Panting, heart burning,
Keep going, keep going.
Still running.
Pace
Round corners,
Down halls into dead ends.
Shadows catching,
Grabbing, pulling,
Crash, bang,
Run silent!
Free, free like the wind,
But do not turn round.

David Knapton (10)
Hornsea Primary School, Hornsea

Snow

White as clouds
A misty moist wisp
Floating down and turning the concrete into white fluff.
Whirling and hurling down on to the grey stone carpet,
Falls, settles but never ending.
Layers upon layers whizzing down
Cold as a petrified stone
Altering the weather to assemble a storm.
Whimpering as it melts in the sunrise.
White as clouds, a moist misty crisp,
A white blanket wraps up the Earth.

Lisa Brooke (11)
Hornsea Primary School, Hornsea

Thunder And Lightning

T he fluorescent light struck, turned into flames,
H itting the world with its uninvited body,
U nder and over, moving round the Earth.
N ever resting, frantically burning,
D esperately breathing creatures smelling the odour.
E ating away, grasping, hungrily,
R acing people, hiding from the fearful atmosphere.

L icking through the air like a forked tongue
I mmediately striking again at the earth
G reedily shaking, devouring the air
H unting for the next victim
T alking in its own language, chittering, chattering,
N ot worrying about destruction,
I ts gold body spirited out of the darkness
N ight no more, the day has come
G one, calm and at peace.

Harriet Taylor (10)
Hornsea Primary School, Hornsea

Heaven

Wispy clouds, whipped up cream,
Drifting bodies living as on Earth
Radiant ring of light, feathered wings,
Shining gold on amber sun
Dreamy, delicious substance,
Though it cannot be tasted.
A lifeless home
Guarded by divine bodies.
Mortals rest in your dreams . . .
Wispy clouds, whipped up cream.

Ella Rowbotham (11)
Hornsea Primary School, Hornsea

Down In The Cellar

Down in the cellar, the dark dusty cellar
I can see,
My rusty old bicycle
A crate of beer bottles
Fee Fee's old collar
A spider or two
The old bathroom loo
A cot that my dad was supposed to mend
Mouldy old cushions
Baby's old blanket
A picture of the iceberg that sank the Titanic,
And deep in the corner
There is something green
So I run away to my room
No longer that keen!

Anna Railton (11)
Hornsea Primary School, Hornsea

Fire

Flashes of colour
Bombard the sky,
Crashes and explodes with rage.
Orange, cardinal red and amber,
Sparks flying, shooting
An inferno as hot as the blazing sun.
Bright lights filling the atmosphere
Destroying anything that was there before.
The flames licking the air
Feel the stale smoky smell in your mouth -
Falling to the ground, starts to die.
One last effort of erratic splutters,
Nothing but flashes of black dust.
The flashes of colour have gone.

Victoria Walker (11)
Hornsea Primary School, Hornsea

The New Child

No friends,
Nobody to play with,
No one I recognise,
Everybody might hate me,
Everybody ignores my needs,
Everybody walks away,
Children talking,
Children looking at me,
Children walking past me,
Sitting outside on the bench,
Sitting alone,
Sitting alone listening to the noise,
Teachers shouting,
Teachers drinking tea and coffee,
Teachers blowing the whistle,
Someone is coming,
Someone wants to talk to me,
Someone wants to be my friend
At last no more misery,
At last no more being alone,
At last a friend.

Bethany Platten (11)
Hornsea Primary School, Hornsea

The Volcano

Red burning embers, choking throats,
Hot burning fire, sizzles, scorches.
A vermilion inferno licking the terrified rock.

Snap of blistering flames -
Moving quickly, enveloping the hillside.
Exploding roar, terrifying scream,
Smell of suffocating fills the silent air.
It lives in the heart of anger.

Kayleigh Metcalfe (11)
Hornsea Primary School, Hornsea

Oh No! Sats!

They're coming
The dreaded SATs
Teacher talking
Constantly
About SATs, SATs, *SATs*.
I've wondered
What are they?
Are they monsters?
Possibly a dragon?
That waits hiding
Getting ready to strike
On an unexpected victim
A small child?
Scared
Terrified
So he runs
He falls and is attacked by a swarm of SATs.

Will it happen to me?
It may in May.

I wonder!

Marcus Anderson (10)
Hornsea Primary School, Hornsea

Turtle

Glides gently through clear water
Flippers rippling, circling effortlessly.
Bobs its head, like a stripy cork
Popping from the delicate shell.
Oval armoured body with brown-black blotches
Glistens under an azure sky.
Gentle creature, innocent and kind
Glides gently through clear water.

Ailsa Williamson (10)
Hornsea Primary School, Hornsea

Death

The sudden fire of guns
Piercing the air like knives cutting bread,
Getting nearer every second
Impossible to stop!

Once someone's gone, impossible to return.
A black hole in your heart, and mind
Where they have vanished
(I know nothing of death).

I know nothing of death,
I never will until it's upon me.
Grandpa knows . . .
So will I eventually!

Dominic Page (10)
Hornsea Primary School, Hornsea

Midnight

Moon of doom
Stars that fright
The sky is gloomy
Shadow creeping in the moonlight.

Castle so tall
A calm sea
Will I fall?
Head swirling - I can't get free.

Trees rustle - fear
Wind whistling all night
Owls hooting near
The creature crawled into the light.

Ian Adams (11)
Hornsea Primary School, Hornsea

Midnight

Midnight
All is calm, all is still
But there are things looking at you
Floorboards creaking
Windows rattling.

Midnight
Our Grandfather clock strikes twelve
Owls hooting in the distance
Dogs howling in their kennels
Cats fighting and caterwauling
In the middle of the night.

Midnight
Street lamps flickering
Doors creaking below
Twigs crackling and birds shrieking
As the full moon glows
High in the sky
Midnight
All is calm, all is still.
Or is it?

Lauren Page (10)
Hornsea Primary School, Hornsea

A Hot Summer's Day

Burns, boils, scolds and spits
Pierces like a polished bullet
Crisp, fresh grass soaks up the rays
Wind whispers to itself
As it invites the warmth to play.
Sea polishing the sand
Under the comforting arms
A clear sky
Silently tiptoes in a pillow of soft feathers.

Becki Johnson (11)
Hornsea Primary School, Hornsea

Chocolate

Chunk at a time
Melting deliciously,
Dances and plays
In a riot of sugar.
Explodes like a fountain
And softly slips away.

Chunk at a time,
Mouth waters
In anticipation
For the next brown velvet treat.

Slowly, carefully,
Savour the final chunk.
Lips licked, lips smacked,
Pure delight!

Alice Hackney (10)
Hornsea Primary School, Hornsea

Midnight

Clock strikes
Repeating beats.
New day arises
Like a phoenix
From the ashes.

A heartbeat ticks
Endlessly continues,
Striking faintly
In the dark, cold corridor
Of the silent house.

Molly Stephenson (11)
Hornsea Primary School, Hornsea

Unsure

Dripping water black, blue
Wind whistling a mournful tune
Sheet lightning spread like soft butter.

Water ripples like black jelly
All the animals scram and scurry
Rain hits the water like bullets
Thunder roaring and lightning hits.

Clouds muster and hove above
Trees giving each other a gentle shove
Rain falling, lightning clatters
Trees scarred and shattered.

Creeping footsteps, a shiver down my spine
I think I just broke the line
Stars floating in the midnight sky
Moon watching the stars go by.

James Walker (10)
Hornsea Primary School, Hornsea

The Nightmare

Darkness, darkness, everywhere
There's a door, do I dare?
Open, it's open, no turning back.
Bang! The door shuts, all turned black.
Screaming, yelling, laughing too,
Voices shouting, 'What's wrong with you?'
Evil eyes pierce and stare
In this bleak, black nightmare.
Darkness, darkness, everywhere
There's a door, yes I dare!

Joe Cox (11)
Hornsea Primary School, Hornsea

Nearly Lunchtime

Open eyed children
Pushing and shoving
The smells taunting them
Another everlasting queue
Smells swiftly making its way up nostrils
Annoying them
Tormenting them
Dinner ladies stand hand in hand with deadly weapons
Spoon and a fork
Serving
>Horrible custard
>Sticky pudding
>Brick chips
>And other selections from their specially prepared
>>Children's menu!

Glen Breary (10)
Hornsea Primary School, Hornsea

Midnight

As the sky is fading away
The house of horror looms
Dark trees talking with fear
Shadows creeping through the doom
Creaking doors swing to and fro
Owls hooting with a creepy crow.

Moonlight shines eternally from up high
Stars shooting through the sky
Dripping water, trickling blood
Standing in a pile of mud
The wind is getting warmer now
But will I never know how.

Ben Henderson (11)
Hornsea Primary School, Hornsea

Wide Awake

Shhh!
All is calm, all is night
Woken up, by the silence around me,
Birds roost, all is now motionless,
No sounds, only the whispering of the trees
Everyone is asleep
. . . But I'm awake.
Wide awake!
Snores creeping down the corridor,
Sitting there, listening to the chime of the
grandfather clock strike 12
The beam of the moon shining on my face
No one is up
But I'm
Wide awake!

Joseph Sullivan (10)
Hornsea Primary School, Hornsea

Midnight

Owls hooting under the evil sparkling stars
Dark trees rustling and swaying fiercely
In the spooky woods with no people or cars
The silver moon is shining sleeplessly.

Stars floated in the cold dark sky
Sweat rushing down my body
The moon shone eternally from up high
I thought I was the last.

Shadows creeping tree to tree
Thinking they are after me!
Too much scary gloom
Rumbles of horrible doom.

Jak Kershaw (10)
Hornsea Primary School, Hornsea

Four In The Morning

The clock strikes four
The heating groaning loudly
The wind whistling lightly
Hamsters on the noisy wheel spinning
Cats fighting for their territory
The tree branches fighting to get in the open window
Four in the morning
Mum is snoring
Dad's on the toilet
It's nearly time for work
Creaking down the rickety stairway
Silent like it should be
Tiptoeing to the door
Be quiet
I take a look to make sure it's clear
Flocks of birds fly over like big clouds floating
Milk bottles clash together bang! Bang!
The milkman on his early rounds
The clock ticking
Back to sleep.

Rebecca Moir (11)
Hornsea Primary School, Hornsea

Midnight

As I was walking along the street
The church clock struck twelve
The shadows crept across the sky
As noisy traffic passed me by.

Owls creep out and make loud noises
Foxes hunt for food
Stars twinkle and glitter
And the smoke smells bitter.

Danielle Davison (10)
Hornsea Primary School, Hornsea

Up In The Attic

Up in the attic I can see . . .

Boxes piled to the top with old junk
A doll's house missing a roof
Newspaper dating back to the sixties
Mum's prom dress
Dad's snapped records
Gran's false teeth
And a photo of my best friend in a wooden
pink frame.

A box full of cans waiting to be recycled
My brother's first nappy, *yuk!*
An ashtray that Dad made at school
My Hallowe'en costume
Grandad's medals
A holey tent
And a photo from school from when I was seven.

Oh yes,
I almost forgot
Lots and lots of bats!

Hannah Watson (11)
Hornsea Primary School, Hornsea

Midnight Fever

The bed shook with a sudden bang
I rushed towards the window up I sprang
Stars were glistening in the sky
I heard a voice breathe in my ear
'You. You're going to die.'
I felt dizzy wandering in fear
Soon I realised he was near,
It was not a scary dream
I gave out a piercing scream.

Michael McNeil (10)
Hornsea Primary School, Hornsea

Midnight Dream

Midnight, midnight,
All around the world,
Ghosts come out,
And they sound absurd.

Blackening sky
Horror looming
House is gloomy
Darkness that is exaggerating.

Although it's dark,
My vision is clear,
I have no idea,
Of what you may fear.

Ghouls and ghosts,
A spider's web,
Witches too,
A trap for you.

Sean Howcroft (10)
Hornsea Primary School, Hornsea

Midnight Stroll

Creeping along the corridor
Dark, misty, gloomy gore.

People whispering
Someone screeching.

Smell of mud . . .
. . . Maybe it's *blood!*

Heart's thumping
Eyeballs jumping.

I crept along the corridor
Dark, misty, gloomy, gore!

Andrew Barr (11)
Hornsea Primary School, Hornsea

What's Your Excuse Today?

Tuesday
Awful Tuesday
I don't like Tuesday.

Dad
Please Dad
I don't feel very well Dad.

Rush
Need to rush
I really have to rush.

Clothes
Need some clothes
Have to wear clothes.

Breakfast
Need breakfast
Must eat breakfast.

School
Don't like school
Don't want to go to school.

Saturday
'It's Saturday' said Dad
Thank goodness it's Saturday.

Jade McKenzie (10)
Hornsea Primary School, Hornsea

Midnight

Ghost came out at midnight
Running all around the sky
Wolves whistling, foxes running
Moonlight shining on the grass
Stars shine overhead like glass.

Stuart Green (10)
Hornsea Primary School, Hornsea

Death

Screaming, scratching,
'Let me out!'
Tortured faces all about,
Deepest dungeons,
Rotting skulls,
A raising knife - danger pulls.
Scarlet canvas on the floor,
Strange signs written on the door,
Wilting flowers,
Withered trees,
People kneeling on two knees,
An axe, chopping for the win,
Twisted faces closing in . . .
Cloth of darkness around your head,
You're alone in darkness, asleep in bed.
People shout at you in rage
You're in the nightmare, trapped in a cage.

Charlotte Ridley (11)
Hornsea Primary School, Hornsea

Tornado

Thrash, smash, thrash, smash,
It destroys as it roars
Everything in its path
Twisting, turning,
An enormous spiral
Of anger and rage
Devours like a hungry beast.
Shouting, screaming, children crying.
Noise fading, shouts quietly,
No more crying, sun rising.
Silence - no noise.
Children laughing,
Mums sighing,
Calm, peace, calm, peace.

Ben Cooper (11)
Hornsea Primary School, Hornsea

Wet Playtime

Chairs clanging and falling over,
Girls giggling at funny stories from their friends
Boys running around
Out of control, endlessly,
The sound of the games cupboard opening.

People running in and out of the classroom
One to get juice, one to go to the toilet
The sound of rain drizzles down the window,
Piles of games,
Collapse, fall on the floor
As girls talk about how they would love to have their hair!

Wet playtime is almost over,
Girls get together their points chart and pencils
Boys put their little skateboards back in their drawers
Everyone leaves
To their next lesson
As they say goodbye to their friends until lunchtime.

Playtime is completely over
The madness from the corridors has gone to quiet
Children sit down at their desk in English
Reading books
Are opening to the right page
As the teacher goes around the classroom
And makes sure we are being quiet.

Annie Hilton (10)
Hornsea Primary School, Hornsea

My Grandad's Attic

I can see
Mouldy sandwiches which have been there for weeks
Crumpled up photographs of me and my brother
It's like a freezer up here
So cold, so damp
Squashed newspapers down the side of a chair
Smell of smoke
I can't bear it
Strange noises like someone's spying on me
My dad's battered punchbag
Hanging from the ceiling
An old pair of my grandad's glasses
Still trying to remember him
Maybe he's watching
Here in his attic.

Jamie Wright (12)
Hornsea Primary School, Hornsea

Down In The Cellar

Down in the cellar I can see . . .
Bags of mouldy potatoes and mucked up coal
Cracked wine bottles
Dinted beer cans
Smashed picture frames
Fingerprinted photos of when I was younger
Old videos with all their insides taken out.

Grandad's old smelly slippers
And cracked glasses with no lenses
Then suddenly on the floor I see a bunch of mice
Munching some old rotten cheese
I think I'd better leave now.

Joe Williams (10)
Hornsea Primary School, Hornsea

What's Your Excuse Today?

'Late again I see,'
My teacher's eyes burning into me,
'What's your excuse today?
I won't believe you whatever you say.'
'Well sir,

The heavens opened and I suddenly saw *God,*
But then monsters got me
Like a giant haddock or cod
They put creatures all over my head
Sucked out my brain
Then I woke up in bed
Yes sir.

It was a dream you see
My teacher's eyes staring into me

I'm sorry I say
But that's my excuse for today!

Taylor Giles (11)
Hornsea Primary School, Hornsea

Midnight

Stars floated in the midnight sky
Images fluttering like trembling butterflies
Dark shadows creep upon me
Wind whistling, howling, stirring the sea.

Trees blow with the midnight flow
Doors open to and fro
Birds tooting
Owls hooting
I can't see where to go.

Matthew Roberts (10)
Hornsea Primary School, Hornsea

Nearly Lunchtime!

My tummy rumbles
It's nearly lunchtime
I hear the noise of children pushing their chairs under -
The desks
Oh the smell
Of
Turkey burgers
Gorgeous chips
And lovely sweet sticky puddings and custard.

My mouth drops open and my nose wrinkles
As I stare out of the window
Everybody is rushing out of their classroom
To a choice
Of
Lamb tender, steak
Lovely spaghetti Bolognese
And chocolate crunch. Yum-yum.

My eyes grow bigger
I rush to the line to get in first
We finally get in -
The delicious food display
Of
A jumbo sausage
Mash potatoes
Angel whirl.

My tummy rumbles
It's nearly lunchtime
Heaven!

Lucy Wallwork (10)
Hornsea Primary School, Hornsea

Down In The Cellar

Down in the dark, dingy cellar
I can see . . .
Rats running about squeaking
All around me
Bats fluttering, dodging spiders hanging from the ceiling
Cobwebs dangling in corners
Moss on the walls
All green and fluffy like nature's velvet
Wallpaper all damp and soggy
Cracks appearing on the walls
Boxes piled on top of each other
Filled with bottles of old sour wine
Dust on everything my eyes make contact with
I can smell the odour of rotten eggs.
Down in the cellar I saw . . .
I saw things that would make any human cringe
The smell of things, I never want to smell again
The feel of slimy mould that I never want to have to experience again
I leave the room
My mind full
Of the stench
Down in the cellar.

Ashleigh Robinson (11)
Hornsea Primary School, Hornsea

Lightning And Thunder

The lightning hit against my window,
Crashing the windowpanes backwards and forwards.
It cluttered against the ground,
Clashing against the windows.
Dark at night the lightning comes back,
Immediately the thunder hits the top of the trees,
Crashing on the ground.
The lightning battered against the walls,
Coming back at night.

Hannah Rawson (10)
Hornsea Primary School, Hornsea

The Eclair

Creamy, mouth-watering
Chocolatey, flavoursome
And ever so tasty.

People cry just to taste them
Even die in order to devour them!
Marching the campaign
Can it be eaten with champagne?

The cream in the centre
Like a void in which to enter.
It drives me round the bend
Will it ever end?

Creamy, buttery, mouth-watering
Slips gently down
Yum!

Kevin Button (10)
Hornsea Primary School, Hornsea

Wolf

Howls under the deep dark moon,
Cuts through the darkness
With eerie squeals like an animal trapped in pain
Longing for the light of morning.
A sleek, sly animal watching, waiting.
Protecting her young
Through the long silent night.
Smells the air for danger,
Smells the air for the scent of humans -
Hunting humans.
Tenderly licks her infants
As they huddle together
Under daylight.

Joseph Singleton (10)
Hornsea Primary School, Hornsea

Home Time At School!

Chairs clatter,
Pushing and shoving
From impatient children
Eager to get out of
School, boys darting through
The crowds, as girls 'chatter'.
Secondary pupils stood waiting for their mums
To collect their kids.
Bangs and slams from Year 5 downstairs
Lunch boxes kicked about
Then the teachers start to shout
Then sudden silence . . . they're all gone
Only a few sounds are heard,
Clank of keys as the caretaker locks up the school
Cleaner sweeps the floor . . . and . . .
Boiler keeps on clanking
As we close the classroom door
Letters just left by the ones who just don't care
Another school day has ended, aren't we all aware!

Mollie Thompson (11)
Hornsea Primary School, Hornsea

Lunchtime!

Children restless, puffed out,
Waiting for the endless queue to break down
Pushing and shoving
Miss screaming for silence
But it won't come.

Smells attracting their attention
Jumping up and down in front of the window continuously
Smells so delicious
Boys teasing girls, annoying them.
Food at last.

Sam Hayden (10)
Hornsea Primary School, Hornsea

My Cousins

This is the tall one, older and wiser
Maybe she's four but she's been here before
Elegant and graceful
She dances around
Playing fairies and pixies
In her fairy-tale world
She is the princess
In her pink little dress
For pink is the colour she likes best
Her crown of jewels
Shines as bright as her eyes
She lights up a room when full of gloom.

This one is smaller
At only two years
But certainly makes up for the lack of years
She marches around for she is the boss
Stamping her feet
Because Winnie's the best
She sees no one else
As she breaks into song
Clapping her hands as she sings along
A bubble of happiness
Is this little one
Like a breath of fresh air
She sweeps you along
Away to the land far beyond
These are my diamonds, my treasures for life
One is calm the other the storm
Put them together and happiness wins
With these two little ones.

Lauren Deakin (11)
Kingsway Primary School, Goole

My Imagination

Need For Speed is my favourite game
When I can't do it I get mad
But when I can do it I am glad
I try and beat my brother but I never do
It is good because my car is better
And faster than his too
The growls and groans of engines
Make my heart beat faster
When my car crashes it feels like a disaster
The colours, lights and sounds are so exciting
I sit on the edge of my seat
Ooh it's so nail-biting
I am happy and I am sad but either way I am glad
That I have got this game to play
To play, to play all of any other day.

Christopher Masterman (10)
Kingsway Primary School, Goole

The Snowy Day

The snow laying on the ground
Snowballs shaped all round
Shoe prints trailing along the path
Leading to a melting snowman
The snow falling on the trees
Sparkling white as diamonds
Children playing and getting wet knees
And people having fun
Sledges sliding across the snowy white hill.

Rebecca Quarmby (10)
Kingsway Primary School, Goole

Football

A cold, chilly morning
Arrive at the field
Changing into our kit
Girls chatting, but nervous too
Sound of studs on the concrete
We run up to the pitch
Coach shouts 'Come on girls,
Time to warm up.'
Running, stretching, jumping high
Practising ball skills
Whistle blows
Game begins
Good footwork and passes
Tackling the opposition
The ball goes down the pitch
Passing to and fro
It's Abbie like a whippet
She shoots
It's a goal!
The girls go wild, along with the crowd
But we must keep focused
It's a great game
Goole playing the best
More tackles, more goals
Kit muddy with dirt
Whistle blows
We've won
Excited and proud
Dirty kits thrown in bag
Girls socialise with team spirit
Ready for the next game.

Megan Garland (10)
Kingsway Primary School, Goole

The Men In Black

The men in black
Undercover agents
In a secret location
Saving our nation
From alien invasion
Gadgets and gizmos
Help them to find
Any alien
That get out of line.

Any strange activity
They're first on the scene
Guns ablazing
Aliens crazing
Back at HQ
The aliens in tow
Meddlesome monsters
No more.

The people in the street
Have their memories erased
They see a white flash
Which leaves them in a daze
Home they go
To have a rest
Wake in the morning
What a strange dream!

Back at HQ
Everyone congratulating you
You've passed the test
Now you're one of the best
Let's get some more aliens!

Luke Patchett (10)
Kingsway Primary School, Goole

The School Bully

The school bully is called Paul,
And he thinks he's really tough
He keeps on slapping my head
He keeps on nicking our stuff
But who cares what that creep says?
Because tonight he will pay
For all his evil ways
When he puts on his wellies
To rush home for his tea,
He will find them full of water.
Sorry, but I was dying for a wee!
He is lucky I didn't need a poo.
I weed in them because I couldn't find a loo.
Paul ranted and raved,
We laughed all the same
His feet were all wet
The teacher just said 'Oh what a shame!'
I never told anyone what I had done
It felt good to get him back
Without getting the blame
He's been nice since that day,
Paul's quiet, he's just not the same . . .

Dallas Woods (10)
Kingsway Primary School, Goole

The Serpent Glides

The serpent glides in the night
Giving sailors a fright
During the day, it sleeps in a cave
But when it wakes
It sends ships to a watery grave
And when sailors survive
It attacks and eats their brains.

Adam Hairsine (10)
Kingsway Primary School, Goole

Deep Blue Sea

Sailing, sailing across the sea
People getting seasick
A storm comes over
We pull up the anchor
The fish swim away into the
Deep blue sea!
The sea goes dark blue
The waves crash against the boat
People are scared of sinking
to the mystery below.

James Sharpe (10)
Kingsway Primary School, Goole

Hate

Hate as red as raging bull's eyes
Hatred like the harsh sound of a gun being fired
Tastes of red-hot chilli peppers
It feels like a pin, deeper and deeper in your skin,
It smells like burning rubber right under your nose.

Thomas Ansell (11)
Kirmington CE Primary School, Kirmington

Love

Love is as red as a rose
The sound of bells ringing
The smell of Christmas pudding
It feels just like soft velvet
It tastes like melted chocolate.

Lauren Roberts (9)
Kirmington CE Primary School, Kirmington

The Perfect Wedding

Lovely wedding dresses
No hair in messes
Confetti on the floor
Then I saw bridesmaids
Pretty in the sun
Having lots of fun.
Lovely flowers pretty and white
Bouquet in the air
Oh what a sight!

Lillie Laverick (9)
Kirmington CE Primary School, Kirmington

Fear

Fear as black as a midnight sky,
The screeching of children crying,
Tastes of salt, dry and harsh,
It feels sharp and rusty as barbed wire,
The stench of death.

Nicholas Cassidy (11)
Kirmington CE Primary School, Kirmington

Love

Love is as red as a rose
The sound of sweet birds singing
The taste of melting chocolate
It feels like the sunshine's rays
It smells of pansies in a meadow.

Chloe Rear (9)
Kirmington CE Primary School, Kirmington

Ice Cream

Ice cream is soft and cold,
It gives a smooth, softening feel
To the back of the throat
Beautiful ice cream
I love ice cream
Bubbles all went pop
Sliding around my mouth.

Aaron Woods (8)
Kirmington CE Primary School, Kirmington

Happiness

Happiness is soft, silky pink,
Sounds like sweet bluebirds singing.
Tastes like melted chocolate running down your throat.
It feels like warm water all over your body,
It smells like fresh new roses.

Joanne Watson (9)
Kirmington CE Primary School, Kirmington

Bravery

Bravery as blue as the night sky
The sound of a person standing up to their fears
The taste of sweet revenge
Feels like the cold silver of a knight's armour
The smell of your fear coming towards you.

Sam Thompson (10)
Kirmington CE Primary School, Kirmington

Love

Love is as red as a rose
Tastes of strawberries and cream
Feels like a silky ribbon surrounding me
Sounds like a bell tingling around me
Smells like sweet summer air.

Shannon Bailey (9)
Kirmington CE Primary School, Kirmington

The Fish

As tiny as your boot,
Sharks are frightening but cute
Fish can swim fast and zoom
They swim as fast as a witch's broom
The fish swim really fast
And they always have a blast
Fish are shiny as gold.

Megan Bell (8)
Longhill Primary School, Hull

The Fish

They are as slippery as ice
As fast as a zooming rocket
They are as colourful as a rainbow
They are squashy like a sponge
As sad and as dull as orphans
They are wrinkly like grandmas
Fish are as shiny as gold.

Yasmin Cox
Longhill Primary School, Hull

The Fish

They zoom like a rocket
They could swim out of your pocket
They are very colourful
They are very huntable
They are shiny as gold
They will not do as they are told.

Danny Grayson (8)
Longhill Primary School, Hull

The Fish

They feel as scaly as a snake
They zoom as fast as a rocket
Some fish are as smooth as silk
They zoom as fast as lightning.

Naomi McLaren
Longhill Primary School, Hull

The Fish

F is for as fast as thunder
I is for as slippery as ice
S is for shy of people
H is for the hollows where they live.

Darian Francis
Longhill Primary School, Hull

The Fish

Some are colourful like a flower
Some dart through the water with such power
Some are as big as a house
Some are tiny as a mouse.

Brendon Scott
Longhill Primary School, Hull

The Fish

Some fish are very still and stay
Fish move fast to get their prey
Some very brightly shine
Some are very, very fine
They are in the water
Playing with their daughter.

Rebecca Casey (8)
Longhill Primary School, Hull

Frosty Morning

Picnic table
Toadstools
Cold hands and feet
White fence
Spiky grass
Frozen toes
Wet playground
Slippery playground.

Liam Rudd (10)
Longhill Primary School, Hull

The Fish

They are speedier than a motorbike
They shoot fast like a rocket
They are thinner than a piece of rope
They are dazzling like the sun
They are fast like a zooming jet
They go in a flash, splash!

Mathew Headon (8)
Longhill Primary School, Hull

Frosty Morning

Damp pond
Bright sun
Diamond ice
Soggy mud
Crispy leaves
Slipping bark
Frozen picnic table
Frozen toadstools
Bare trees
Frosty wood
Slippery snakes and ladders
Work site building
Icy nursery
Wet, damp
White fence
Roof icy.

Claire Sanderson (10)
Longhill Primary School, Hull

Frosty Morning

Crisp grass
Slippery playground
Ripped toadstools
Shy pixies
Slippery bark
Crispy leaves
Frozen wood
Sparkling ice
Shining icicles
Lumpy picnic tables
Cold flowers
Bare trees.

Christopher Wheeldon (10)
Longhill Primary School, Hull

The Fish

They are sloppier than a kiss
More colourful than a rainbow
They are faster than grease lightning
They are always being eaten
They are frightening
They are always fighting
They are very sensitive.

Christopher Strafford (7)
Longhill Primary School, Hull

Snake Kenning

Rough skin
Sharp eyes
Tongue hisser
Hole slider
Tree climber
Ground slitherer
Mouse hunter.

Kye Smith (8)
Newington Primary School, Hull

A Rabbit Kenning

Brown white
Smooth soft
Twitch nose
Leaps hops
Fluffy tail
Pointy ears
Whiskery boy
Playful jumps
Dinky runs.

Abigail Bonehill (9)
Newington Primary School, Hull

My Cat

My cat's eyes are like telescopes
My cat's legs are bony like a tree
My cat's teeth are razor-sharp like a knife
My cat's tail is camouflage like a mud pool
My cat's back is soft like a teddy bear
My cat's whiskers are flexible like a slinky
My cat's legs are like a junction with fleas.

Sophie Greene (9)
Newington Primary School, Hull

Cats

The cat's back is a woolly jumper
The cat's tongue is like a ball of pins
The cat's tail is like a whiteboard rubber
The cat's whiskers are like metal wires
The cat's ears like a fish's tail.

Leah Cochran (7)
Newington Primary School, Hull

Song Of The Plane

You see the smoke at Humberside
It takes off like a speeding bolt
A roaring lion in the sky
It could land like a swooping hawk
It can shine like a golden dart.

Daniel Taylor (8)
Newington Primary School, Hull

Stop, Look, Listen, Live . . .

Stop, look, listen and live
Yeah! Stop, look, listen and live.

Be quiet! Be quiet!
Be quiet in the back of the car.

Do not disturb. Do not disturb.
Do not disturb the person who is driving.

Then the driver. Then the driver.
Then the driver will watch the road.

Yeah! Stop, look, listen, live.
Stop, look, listen, live.

Naomi Hassan (9)
Newington Primary School, Hull

Cats

My cat's head is like a ball of wool
My cat's tail is like a pipe cleaner
My cat's back is like a soft cushion
My cat's eyes are as black as night
My cat's whiskers are a wiry coat hanger
My cat's legs are as bony as me.

Mirza Ibrisimovic (9)
Newington Primary School, Hull

My Cat

My cat's eyes are like marbles
My cat's teeth are sharp razors
My cat's tail is a whip
My cat's back is a spring
My cat's whiskers are barbed wire.

Anthony Arnott (9)
Newington Primary School, Hull

I Would . . . I Wouldn't . . .

I wouldn't do wheelies
In the middle of the road
I wouldn't do that . . .
Not me!
I wouldn't do tricks on the road
I wouldn't do that . . .
Not me!
I wouldn't play chicken across the road
I wouldn't do that . . .
Not me!
I wouldn't run across the road
I wouldn't do that . . .
Not me!

I would wear a seat belt
I would do that . .
Yes me!
I would wear a bike hat
I would do that . . .
Yes me!
I would walk across the road
I would do that . . .
Yes me!
I would ride my bike sensibly
I would do that . . .
Yes me!

Keiran Scholey (10)
Newington Primary School, Hull

Untitled

It curls up near the fire like a fluffy football
It scurries up the tree like a daft monkey
Its whiskers are straight like sticks and feel like wire
It dives from the tree to the ground like a diver
It scratches the bed like digging knives.

Chelsea Clark (8)
Newington Primary School, Hull

Song Of The U-Boat

You see the bubbles at Dover
As big as a blue whale
As agile as a seal
As quiet as a hunting lion
It slides through the waves like a snake.

Alexander Wilson (8)
Newington Primary School, Hull

Winning

Don't be upset if you don't win
Don't chuck it in the bin
As long as you tried
Because once your tears have dried
Put a smile on your face
And act ace!
As long as you enjoyed it . . .

Katie Higham (11)
Old Clee Junior School, Grimsby

Autumn

Some leaves are the colour gold
But the rest well they're just bold.
The silver birch tree is shining in the sun
While the other trees get nothing just breeze.
The leaves are falling off one by one
There will be nothing left to praise.

Amy Hopkinson (10)
Old Clee Junior School, Grimsby

My Ideal Teacher

My ideal teacher is one who listens to me,
He'll teach me all he knows you see.
He's always kind and never gets mad,
If he did the children would go home sad.
They wouldn't want to learn and do their sums,
So round to the school would come their mums.
He'll try to be patient with those that were bad,
He'll say 'It's in your own interest to learn my lad.'
Sometimes we'll give him a headache,
He'd think to himself, *be quiet for goodness sake.*
But with a smile and a grin
He'll forgive us our sin
So then we'll try to not make a din,
So stand up Mr Shaw, it's you I mean,
Keep up the good work and we'll always be keen!

Amy Kearns (11)
Old Clee Junior School, Grimsby

Trenches

The trenches were really wet and muddy
The soldiers were down in the dumps
Their ears were sore and aching
Because of the loud bangs and the bumps.
One soldier was sat down crying
Saying 'Oh when are we going to go home?
Back home to our wives and families
That we've left all faraway and alone?
Here comes another bomb flying
Oh God that one sounds really close.
Please God get us all out of here safely,
And bring this whole war to an end.'

Drew Morgan (9)
Old Clee Junior School, Grimsby

Home Time

I look at the clock,
Oh what a shock!
Twenty past three,
That will do for me.
Home time again,
For a walk down the lane.
Or is it Dad in the car?'
Then I won't have to walk far.
I wonder what's for tea,
Or how long it will be?
Is there time for the PlayStation?
It would fill me with elation.
Oh good a cooked meal,
More time to reveal,
Who is going to be the winner?
While Mum cooks the dinner.

Daniel Stuffin (7)
Old Clee Junior School, Grimsby

Fluffy The Cat

She wakes up in the morning all proud and ladylike
From her corner beyond the steep stairs.
Tail up, chin up
She walks downstairs.
She tiptoes in the kitchen 'n'
Has a scrap with the other cat
(That's Chipstik a little rat, but I still love her)
She goes outside for a little walk
And comes back in for a little fuss
And that's Fluffy our beloved puss.

Daniel Chesman (8)
Old Clee Junior School, Grimsby

Winter Poem

Christmas is nearly here,
Decorations in our home
Keep warm in bed
On our own.

The night we sleep
We think our thoughts
We cannot wait to
See what Santa has brought.

The dog is sleeping
Below the tree
Crimson and hazel,
Robins chirping 1, 2, 3.

Gleaming snow on the ground,
Snowmen dancing outside the door
Rudolph shining his red nose,
We made snow angels on the floor.

Emma Butler (10)
Old Clee Junior School, Grimsby

Special Friend

Valentine's Day is great because I've always got my special mate.
The friends I have I do not hate
But still they are not my special mate.
She's always there when I am sad
And always happy when I am glad.
My time with her is spare
So the good times we enjoy to share.
For the happy times we have together
We know we will always be forever.

Bethany Roberts (9)
Old Clee Junior School, Grimsby

Footie

We're going to the match,
Today is the day,
We're going to win,
Hip hip hooray.

Grimsby v Scarborough
The ball had flown
What a good first half
The whistle has blown.

Grimsby winning 1-0,
Grimsby fans cheering
Scarborough equalise
Now Scarborough are cheering.

Grimsby score again
A minute to go
We'll lose the next match so!

Tom Taylor (9)
Old Clee Junior School, Grimsby

There Is A Tear In My Eye

There is a tear in my eye
Oh why, oh why did they have to die?
A million tears, a single rose,
First the bodies and then the clothes.
Let those little angels play,
While we sit and weep and pray.
Every night we look up into the sky,
We cannot help but mourn and cry.
We miss you already and hope you're not far,
Because in our hearts you will always be stars.

Lucy Webb (11)
Old Clee Junior School, Grimsby

Bedtime

Bedtime in my house
Should be as quiet as a mouse
Instead I can hear . . .
The central heating boiler whirr,
The ring of the phone,
And my dad coming home.
As I lay in my bed,
Thinking of all that's been said,
Thoughts of my day,
Won't go away.
Sometimes that's good,
Others, I wish they would.
My teddy is so tired,
I expect that's what's required.
I know in the morning
It will be me who'll be yawning,
Teddy will be OK,
He can stay in bed all day.
Me, I've got to go to school,
Or at least that's the rule.

Hannah Stuffin (9)
Old Clee Junior School, Grimsby

Autumn Poem

Autumn cones fallen off trees
Bright red berries grow on the trees
Helicopters grow for kids to have fun.

Conkers fall to make new trees
Kids pick them up to play and have fun
Leaves crunch under my feet when I walk on them.

Dawn Spurrell (9)
Old Clee Junior School, Grimsby

Discos And Parties

I went to a disco on Monday
It was so good it was a fun day
I wore a glittery, glamorous dress
It was washed with Lenor and it smelt fresh.

On Tuesday I went to a ball
And my friend met a boy called Paul
Wednesday I went to a party
Met a girl whose name was Martie.

On Thursday I went to a dance
Competitions I have a chance
On Friday I chill out
Football comes on shout, shout, shout!

On Saturday I have some spare time
So I sit down and learn to mime
On Sunday I visit my nanna
And she said 'What a nice bandana'.

That's my week.

Shelby Fountain (9)
Old Clee Junior School, Grimsby

Football Match

Going to the footie match to watch Grimsby Town
Will they win, or will they lose again, like normal?
Twenty five mins into the game my belly says 'Give me food!'
So I go and get a steak pie and a nice hot drink.
When I get back I look at the score board *Yes* 1-0!
At half-time we're 1-0 up, everybody goes to the canteen,
Second half is on, it's time to sit down, Grimsby make a sub,
Macca off, Croac on, that's good.
It's all over, we've won 1-0.
Now home for a nice hot bath.

Joshua Chester (9)
Old Clee Junior School, Grimsby

Fairy Tale

Once upon a time a long time ago,
Were dragons, wizards and kings
There lived a bad witch, with her cat,
And lots of wonderful things,
Like a red frog, a magic spell,
And a huge purple wig.
Then you think of the giant, who lives in the clouds,
Well on top to be precise.
He loves his sausages, eggs and beans,
And also likes his rice.
His wife was beautiful, had long blonde hair,
Her name was Emily Slice.
She was a butcher, chopped little children,
And not-so-big adults for laughter.
'Why do it for laughter, when you can do it for money?'
Said her gigantic gaffer,
They sold so many, she could retire,
And they lived happily ever after.

Hollie Barber (10)
Old Clee Junior School, Grimsby

The Tricky Wizard

Fun-loving wizard, crafty and tricky
With spells up his sleeves and stuffed up his chimney,
Nice cute cats and scary black bats
They all live together in a crumbly brick flat.

With stars on his hat and moons on his socks,
His hair that needs brushing and spots that need squashing,
Tears in his cloak and a wand that needs polishing
The wizard's all lonely and needs some fun loving.

He feels all alone in his cold brick flat
It's covered in cobwebs and this and that,
Now feeling so lonely he hopes there's a chance,
He can meet someone similar for magic and romance.

Fay Sewell (10)
Old Clee Junior School, Grimsby

The Four Seasons

The first of which,
The flowers grow
They start to bud
The petals show.

Then comes hot times
Flowers dry and weep
Then when watered
They begin to leap.

Now the times are very chilly
Leaves begin to fall off trees
Flowers flop
And begin to crease.

The sun's not out
It's cold outside
Snow is falling
All the plants have died.

Alex Revell (11)
Old Clee Junior School, Grimsby

My Teacher

My teacher is still in bed
Sends her pets instead
The monkey to do the register
The giraffe to do the jobs
The parrot to do the maths lesson
The snakes to do the science lesson
And the zebra to do music
And the teacher said 'You did such a good job,
I'll send you back tomorrow!'

Hannah Wright (10)
Old Clee Junior School, Grimsby

The Kite

When the wind blows
Up the kite goes
Whisking and prancing
Frisking and dancing
High, high in the sky!
Lovely green kite like a big leaf swirling,
Twirling and whirling,
High, high in the sky.

When the wind drops,
Down the kite flops,
Wheeling and shifting,
Reeling and drifting
Down, down to the ground
Lovely green kite, like a big leaf dipping,
Flipping and slipping
Down down to the ground!

Jessica Salkeld (11)
Old Clee Junior School, Grimsby

My Ideal Teacher

I guess you think you know my teacher,
You don't you know, he really is a lovely creature,
He makes science fun and good to do,
Even maths and English are easy too.
The best is yet to come,
He is unique, he is the one.
He taught us rugby and hockey too,
There isn't anything he can't do.
He comes to school dressed all smart,
But always looks a mess after art.
So now you know what my ideal teacher would be,
He's the best teacher in the world, wouldn't you agree?

Charlotte Pleasants (9)
Old Clee Junior School, Grimsby

Journey Of A Water Particle

In the freezer, all was still
Me and my friends sat in cold ice-cube trays
I was a little water particle you see,
Oh, I was desperate to be free in so many ways.

Then came the wonderful bright light of freedom
All of a sudden a small pink hand reached in so fast
I hadn't a clue what was happening to me
Then I realised, I was really free at last!

Suddenly . . . *bang!* And I tumbled into a small, round glass,
Then the pink hand was distracted and just left me there,
It was warm in the transparent cup, I didn't want to be free anymore,
Would I live, or would I evaporate into thin air?

No, this was me, a water particle, I thought, *I can survive*
It was then that I realised I was slowly melting, it wasn't a lie.
I was too weak to fight the power of warmth,
And now, on this summer's day I was going to die.

Then the pink hand returned and saw me, no longer alive
The hand picked up the glass and tipped the contents on the outside
floor.
I found myself trickling down the slabs of the busy street,
Where was I going? It was a mystery to me, I didn't know anymore.

Plop! I had fallen into the gutter, and I was now in a small puddle.,
The dirty, cold puddle left me feeling unclean,
It was terrible in there, could anything save me?
Whatever had done this to me was incredibly mean!

I was now really in doubt, I needed a miracle but then . . .
I suddenly experienced something new once again.
I was invisible! Then I floated up gently to the clouds above,
Then when the time was right, I fell down as rain.

Harriet Dales (10)
Old Clee Junior School, Grimsby

Autumn Dream

A wonderful sunflower that's holding onto the last
Threads of summer.
Spraying its magical powers over everybody.

A holly tree with berries as juicy as red lips,
Kissing people in crimson-red juice
With its wonderful gaze.

A silver birch tree that shines like silver coins
Making people cheerful as they admire its beauty.
What a wonderful autumn dream.

Grant Zeebroek (9)
Old Clee Junior School, Grimsby

My School

The teachers don't rule in my school
The kids are totally cool
When the teachers are mad
We're never ever sad.

Us kids are the top of the top
The best of the best
After a day with us
They'll need a long long rest!

Lewis Watson (9)
Old Clee Junior School, Grimsby

Autumn

Autumn is bright and the leaves are light
Red and brown and they fall to the ground
The whistling wind and crunchy leaves red and brown
Making them crumble on the ground.

Amy Coleman (8)
Old Clee Junior School, Grimsby

My Mum

My mum is cool
She looks even cooler in the pool
She has a lovely smile
Even down the shopping aisle
I kiss her goodnight
And turn off the light
And says 'Snuggle up tight,
And have sweet dreams tonight.'

Claire Croft (11)
Old Clee Junior School, Grimsby

My Dog

My dog is fat
My dog is slow
My dog is silly
My dog is smelly
My dog is funny
I love my dog so much!

Josh Barley (8)
Old Clee Junior School, Grimsby

My Bird

My bird is pretty
My bird is colourful
My bird is small
My bird can talk
My bird shall sing and wake me up
And say good morning.

Lewis Patterson (10)
Old Clee Junior School, Grimsby

My Poem

I love you, I love you
I love you so well
If I had a skunk
I would give you a smell.

If I were a witch
I would give you a fright
If I were a dog
I would give you a bite.

If I were a bath tub
I would give you a splash
If I were a fungus
I would give you a rash.

I love you, I love you
So much that I wouldn't
Tell a lie
I promise we'll marry the day that I die!

Kerrigan Brown (9)
Old Clee Junior School, Grimsby

I Like The Snow

I like the snow
It's such a blow
Snowflakes glow
Just like a
Shining moon.

I like the snow
It's such a shame
It has to go.
It's like shimmering diamonds
On the windowsill.

I like the snow
It's such a blow!

So let's celebrate in the snow.

Callum Vick (9)
Old Clee Junior School, Grimsby

The Cow

The friendly cow, all red and white
I love with all my heart.
She gives me cream with all her might
To eat with an apple tart.

She wanders lowing here and there,
And yet she cannot stray,
All in the pleasant open air,
The pleasant light of day.

And blown by all the winds that pass
And wet with all the showers
She walks among the meadow grass,
And eats the meadow flowers.

Keane Boothby (10)
Old Clee Junior School, Grimsby

PlayStations

PlayStations rule but are so cool,
I wish we had one at school.
But I can't wait until the bell goes
When I put on my coat and hat and start walking home,
To play my favourite games.

'Cell Damage', 'Charlie's Angels', 'Pac-man 2',
I always get on to the last level, do you?
Then I play game after game,
Only breaking off to do my homework,
Maths, reading, and my history project again,
As soon as I'm finished, quick as a flash,
I'm back on my PlayStation.
Yes! I'm a winner again.

Paul Cole (9)
Old Clee Junior School, Grimsby

Sweep's Day

Sweep wakes up early in the morning
It's been a long, hard night and he still keeps yawning
He starts to miaow as if to say 'let me in'
I open the door and he's sat on the bin
He jumps right down and walks straight past
I know what he wants it's his breakfast.
I walk to the cupboard to get him some food
And if I don't hurry he'll go in a mood.
We fill up his bowl right up to the top
If he gets any fatter he's likely to pop
When he has finished he still isn't happy
He really is a miserable chappy
He walks into the room and jumps on the chair
He's feeling much happier now 'cause he's starting to purr
He sprawls himself out and is soon fast asleep
That is the story of my cat, Sweep.

Bethany Webb (9)
Old Clee Junior School, Grimsby

Spring

Winter now is over
And it will soon be spring
When all the snowdrops and daffodils
Come out
And the birds begin to sing.
The trees begin to blossom
The grass is nice and green
The nights are getting lighter
So more of nature can be seen
The lambs are in the fields
The chicks are in their nest
This is my favourite season,
The one I like the best.

Sophie Lewis (7)
Old Clee Junior School, Grimsby

Pogo-Mary

My name is Pogo-Mary
My pogo stick goes up and down
My pogo stick goes round and round
I practise on my pogo stick, it's bouncier than ever.

My pogo stick bounces everywhere
Around the garden without a care
Once I bounced so high I landed
In a pond as I jumped one handed.

My clothes got wet and I was cold
Then I found the fish were gold
I climbed out the pond
With clothes soaking wet
Then called in for dinner
I ate and I ate.

I changed my clothes and outside I went
With delight and glee
Then I bounced around the patio
One, two, three . . .

Jessica Norfolk (7)
Old Clee Junior School, Grimsby

My Family

I know my family is rather loud,
But in a way that makes me feel proud,
When we're together,
It feels like forever,
When I have tears,
They take away my fears,
Whenever I'm there,
Whoever I'm with
I'll walk with pride
With my family by my side.

Elizabeth Summers (9)
Old Clee Junior School, Grimsby

Under The Sea

Under the water calm and cool,
Crabs and starfish lay in the rockpool,
Jellyfish stinging with rays on their bodies
Bright coloured fish, orange and blue.

Grey types of sharks swimming away
Swimming away, had enough today.

Sky and sea fill the air
The fish and whales daring to share
Ocean fills the great big world
Eels and crabs carefully curled.

The clam showing off its pearls
The jellyfish swimming
With his legs in curls
The shark runs free
King of the sea.

Wind is smooth and silky
The water frees the rocks
Calm and cool the ocean locks.

Sophie Dolan (10)
Old Clee Junior School, Grimsby

Water

The ice-cap slowly melts and drips,
Tall icebergs float amongst tall ships,
From Arctic wastes the waters flow,
To make the seas and oceans grow.

Tempests, tides and roaring waves,
Have carved out arches, cliffs and caves,
Water creaks and shapes the land,
From mountain range to grain of sand.

Khloe-Celia Jennings (10)
Old Clee Junior School, Grimsby

Little Bird

Little bird flying high, little bird up in the sky
He flutters through the wind and staggers in the air
Bristling his hair.
Whistle, whistle, flying high,
Whistle whistle in the sky.

That's the bird
I want to be . . .

Teresa Shortland (10)
Old Clee Junior School, Grimsby

A Star

I have a little star, they call her peep, peep, peep
She wades the waters deep, deep, deep.
She climbs the mountains high, high, high
Poor little creature
She has but one eye!

Jessica Wortley (8)
Old Clee Junior School, Grimsby

My Racing Car

A super car
Was zooming down the road
It never could be beaten
Because it had no bad
All the other drivers were jealous
Though they were careless
I never ever cheated
Because their cars always overheated
I crossed the line
While they drove into a shrine!

Sam Phillipson (9)
Pasture Primary School, Goole

The Journey Of The River Severn

A boggy pool oozing out of the ground
2000 feet above sea level!
It starts to rain,
And after one year,
Two metres of rain forms a soggy bog.
It dribbles and trickles down the mountains
Slowly but surely.
Flowing downhill taking the long way round,
Instead of the short.
It forms a v-shaped valley.
Then it makes friends with other tributaries at the confluences.
The River Severn approaches the roller coaster waterfall,
'Get ready, hold on tight now!'
Splash!
Into the plunge pool goes the river.
It continues its journey gradually getting faster and faster
It approaches a meander,
And flows across its floodplain,
Dropping off stones that it had picked up earlier
in its journey.'
Are we there yet?' cries the river.
'Nearly, nearly!' replies the sea.
Finally the River Severn reaches its destination
And starts the watercycle again.

Daniel Graves (10)
Pasture Primary School, Goole

Rain

Raindrops on your nose,
With the wind it blows, blows, blows,
Rain mist in the air,
Mist and wind wets your hair.
Downpour, drizzle, mist or shower,
Whatever the weather, I love rain!

Joshua Oldridge (9)
Pasture Primary School, Goole

The Sound Collector

(Based on 'The Sound Collector' by Roger McGough)

A stranger called this morning
Dressed all in black and grey
Put every sound into a folder
And carried them away.

The popping of the popcorn
The purring of the cat
The licking of the ice cream
The yawning of the people
The creaking of the stairs
The flicking of the finger
The frying in the pan
The banging of the door
The whistling of the kettle
The barking of the dogs
The laughing of the hyenas
The wittering of the baby

A stranger called this morning
He didn't leave his name
Left us only silence
Life will never be the same.

Sophie Lloyd (7)
Pasture Primary School, Goole

Pets' Toys

P ets are nice and furry, cute and cuddly
E very time you throw the ball they catch it
T hey are very playful and noisy
S o soft and cuddly.

T hey must be my favourite thing
O ught to be able to talk I think
Y ou must like them
S o soft and cuddly.

Alice Shipley (9)
Pasture Primary School, Goole

My Rabbits That Died

One was grey and one was white
One ran every night.
I went out one morning
The grey one was dead
The white one was alive so I stroked her head.
The grey one was Millie and the white one was Tillie
I loved them both but mine was Millie.
Tillie was fat and Millie was skinny
They liked eating carrots and lettuce too.
I used to let them out some days,
Tillie crawled under the shed
I couldn't get her out.
I left her over night
Then she came out,
I put her in her cage.
One year after Millie died Tillie died too
My sister was sad and so was I.

Samuel Duffin (9)
Pasture Primary School, Goole

Wedding Day

W indy day
E xciting
D addy mad, he can't find his pants
D awn the bride looks beautiful
 I an who is getting married
   is ten minutes late
N anna's crying
G arry my brother is still in bed.

D arren has fallen out of his bed
A bbie the bridesmaid is playing
   on the dance mat
Y uk that's too tight!

Abbie Butler (8)
Pasture Primary School, Goole

The River Severn

There is a boggy pool,
Making its way towards the sea.
Trickling and tumbling over the rocks,
It meets the waterfall,
Going over the bumpy stones.
Rocks falling down and down
Reaching the powerful waters.
It dribbles and flows slowly over
More and more stones.
It starts to dribble faster and faster.

The water cuts making a V-shape valley,
Pebbles rising in the high and low tide,
Swooshing through and through the muddy waters.
The water is swaying left and right,
The journey is about to end,
Flowing into the sea.

Sophie Harrison (11)
Pasture Primary School, Goole

River Journey

As a boggy pool it starts off
Growing slowly.
Grabbing out for its friends
Succeeding
Now its size is growing, growing.

Rapidly it goes,
Like a jockey on a horse,
Eating, demolishing everything in its way.
Finding a short cut down the mountainside
Going even faster.

Then all of a sudden it slows
Comes to a conclusion,
As it spreads its wings,
In search of a new world out at sea.

Grant Bellis (9)
Pasture Primary School, Goole

Journey Of The River Severn

This is how the river starts,
In a boggy pool,
Thousands of feet above sea level
The water is very cool.

Now the water starts to dribble and trickle
Down a muddy slope
Oozing down a grassy hill
Where does it go, I want to know?

Now rivers from far away
Come and combine
Rocks and stones in the sun
How brightly they shine.

Rushing water
Fighting its way down the stream,
Ahead I see the waterfall
Under the sun's beam.

Argh!
Bubble and bubble as I dive
Surfacing from the plunge pool.

Now we carry tonnes of sand
Pebbles and rocks and stones
Meandering, creating a huge flood plain
As huge rocks rub together
It makes a noisy groan.

Now I see, we see, the sea
Heading sharply south,
I see some wildlife
We go into the sea's mouth,
As our journey ends.

Matthew Fenwick (11)
Pasture Primary School, Goole

Journey Of The River Severn

Splish, splash,
Goes the rain tapping on the mountain tops.
It flows down and forms a marshy bog
It's filling up quick, quick, jump
Splash!
It's the spring forming a stream with clear flowing water,
Swerving, dribbling and trickling the water reaches a waterfall.
3, 2, 1, whoosh, it flies off the edge
And flushes down into a plunge pool,
Wearing stones out on the way down.
'Oh look' cries the water, 'An otter!'
The waves swerve past the otter forming a v-shaped valley
When it hits the banks.
The water plunging through the swerving routes.
Finally it reaches its destination.
The sea shining in all its glory
'Hooray' shouts the river 'we are there.'

Matthew Harrison (10)
Pasture Primary School, Goole

The Journey Of A River

Who would have thought that millions of raindrops
could be the source of the river?
So the soggy bog is the beginning it grows into war of water.
Travelling mile after mile, meeting friends as it goes,
they will never break up.
Oh no, what's this? A pile of rocks, argh!
Finally we've passed our first waterfalls,
They are a rough sort of place.
What's this? Another river? It's coming from over there
This has travelled along a v-shaped valley.
Then it turns into a meander,
Rivers stretching their way to the sea.
Finally after hours of hard work they reach the sea.
Ah the life! They scream.

Bethany Wraith (9)
Pasture Primary School, Goole

Journey Of The River Severn

Drip! The rain falls on the hills,
Then collects and soaks into a boggy marsh,
The brown slippery worm of water then travels downwards
Thousands of feet.

Bang! the banks burst and a ferocious river starts its life,
Then flows wildly downhill,
Suddenly another river joins the stream, it's getting bigger now,
Wait a second, look ahead, there's that crashing sound

Rushing down the waterfall down, down it goes,
It crashes into others tumbling, making them fade away,
The water is rushing as it rocks and tumbles,
Then it twists into meanders then floods over the bank side

Finally the river flows roughly to the sea,
Through the estuary where it will restart a new life
In the sea again.

Johnathan Ross-Paterson (11)
Pasture Primary School, Goole

The Course Of A River

A splash of rain, now another.
Oh no! It's all coming down now.
What's this? This is a smiley, sludgy, boggy pool.
Now it's formed its own little stream running down, down
Eventually making a v-shaped valley and running even faster.

It now finds a waterfall, splish! splash!
Falling, falling, the end must be around here somewhere.
Ha, ha, I've found my own little plunge pool.

Whee, whee, I'm meandering round my flood plain
This is ages I've covered my bank again on ho
Yes I've found my delta.
Suddenly, splash, I have reached my end into the sea
Let's do this again!

Liam Watson (10)
Pasture Primary School, Goole

The Sound Collector

(Based on 'The Sound Collector' by Roger McGough)

A stranger called this morning
Dressed all in blue and grey
Put every sound into a sack
And carried them away.

The singing of the birds
The whistling of the kettle
The dripping of the tap
The purring of the cat
The howling of the dog
The bouncing of the ball
The banging on the wall.
The crashing of the fireworks
The popping of the toast
The hissing of the oven
The screaming of the children
The turning of the lock.

A stranger called this morning
He didn't leave his name
Left us only silence
Life will never be the same.

Melissa Leyland (8)
Pasture Primary School, Goole

Vikings

Vikings are scary
Vikings are hairy
Vikings have swords
Sailing through fjords
Vikings have ships
Stealing with whips
Vikings don't lie
They just die.

Luke Kendall (9)
Pasture Primary School, Goole

The Sound Collector

(Based on 'The Sound Collector' by Roger McGough)

A stranger called this morning
Dressed all in blue and grey
Put every sound into a suitcase
And carried them away.

The crunching of the apple
The barking of the pup
The popping of the coke
The smashing of the cup.

The pouring of the water
The miaowing of the cat
The snapping of the tin
The flapping of the mat.

The snoring of the father
The creaking of the door
The banging of the walking stick
The tapping on the floor.

A stranger called this morning
He didn't leave his name
Left us only silence
Life will never be the same.

Thomas Lambert (8)
Pasture Primary School, Goole

The Journey Of The River Severn

I start at the boggy pool
I rush through dykes and rivers
I take parts of the earth with me
I flood little islands
I stop rushing through dykes and rivers
Then I join with other rivers and then I
Meander across its flood plain,
And finally I stop.

Jack Sowerby (10)
Pasture Primary School, Goole

The Journey Of The Severn

There is a boggy pool,
At the top of a hill,
The rain comes down,
And the pool overflows,
It dribbles and trickles,
Down the big, steep hill.

Wider and wider it grows,
Tributaries join, make it grow more,
It hits a waterfall over the rocks,
It carries on expanding as it goes,
Little streams join onto the Severn
Curling as it goes, smoothing rocks as it goes,
This powerful water storm.

The Severn carries on its journey,
Twisting and turning, spinning and swirling,
The journey is coming to an end,
The river meets its ending point,
Ready to flow into the sea.

Adam Scott (9)
Pasture Primary School, Goole

The Bog

Welcome to the cosy, goozy bog, the start of the river,
It becomes wider and wider forming like a river
It flows really fast and slow,
The fish inside have a sparkly glow,
And the wind hushes,
And the river rushes,
And this will be a lovely river,
It will always be forever.

Tanya Boyce (10)
Pasture Primary School, Goole

My Poem About Me!

Drip, drip, I go
Trickling and dripping as well
There I go into a hole
I'm raising, I'm raising, I'm nearly at the top.
I'm the . . .
Splashing and gurgling over the side I go
My friends are just oozing out after me
Through the grassy mountains I go
Digging and digging a v-shaped valley
There I see some old friends coming to join me
Making bigger and bigger
Miles after miles I flow
I look ahead everyone has gone
Suddenly I get the butterflies down, down I fall
I'm falling down a rushing waterfall
I swirl and turn in all directions
I'm picking up small rocks, pebbles and sand as I land
Most annoyingly I suddenly get pushed back and back
I get thrown to the side of the valley
Then I see all the sea one more step
Just one more step
Yes I've made it, I'm finally here
Here I am at my journey's end
I must join my family and friends
And off I go!

Rebecca Naylor (11)
Pasture Primary School, Goole

How The River Started At The River Severn

As I start at the very top,
Just a dribble and a trickle.
I start moving down
Slowly as can be.

I speed up,
Out of his boggy pool.
It's all muddy and tacky,
I can hardly move.

It's like a sucking thing,
That pulls you under.
At last I'm out of this grotty pool,
And into a small world of stream.

There's a lot of longish grass,
That sometimes tickles my face.
Smooth water that's what I like,
No rafts whatsoever.

Now I'm coming up to a wide
Clear watery pool.
It's wide with lots of short grass,
This grass doesn't tickle my face.

It's large with small objects floating about,
Now I'm coming up to a *waterfall*.
Oozing water is now rushing past me,
It's getting faster.

Then splash and crash,
Into the plunge pool.
Now I'm flowing into a meander,
It's curvy and wide.

It also has a mark where earth has been taken away.
Water's flowing faster and before I know it
I'm coming through into the sea mouth.

It's called a delta,
This is where my journey ends.

Jemma Brown (10)
Pasture Primary School, Goole

How A River Starts

A river starts as a boggy pool,
Then starts to get wider and wider,
And starts to flow.
It washes all the earth away,
Then it passes through the v-shaped valley,
Then starts a waterfall there made by slopes on the land,
And the water makes tributaries.
Tributaries are rivers that split into two or more parts.
It passed through the grass, rocks have fallen,
It's getting bigger and bigger and bigger.
It covers the sand that the tide brings in,
It starts to swerve left to right and makes a meander in the river.
I start to make my way to the sea,
The rocks and grass come with me and as we make our way
                                              to the sea,
The tide starts to come in faster and faster
And covers the sandy bank.
Then the ocean's tide comes in between two banks
Down the river making the river higher,
Then settles on the river bed
We finally find our way to the sea.

Amy Nicholls (10)
Pasture Primary School, Goole

My Dog

My dog is always asleep
In front of the fire
She is always growling at people
She always bites people.

Morgan Linnington (9)
Pasture Primary School, Goole

How The River Started

As I start with a drip drop
I drift slowly down the hill.

I start getting faster and suddenly I'm falling
And I am falling down little, small hills,
I am now slowly getting back to my normal speed.

Now I am slowly getting faster,
Oh no another stream is meeting me,
Me and my friend are now going together to the sea.

We are now getting wider and faster,
I think we are coming to an end,
Oh no it seems we are falling down a very steep hill.

Now we are getting wider and,
Slower because we are twisting and turning,
And it is getting harder to move round.

We now can see an opening I think it is the sea,
Yes! Yes! It is the sea, we were right!
Now our journey has ended or has it?
It could just be the beginning.

Charlotte Kenning (10)
Pasture Primary School, Goole

It

It's brown, it's white
It plays in the day and sleeps at night.
It rattles its food and plays with its ball
And it barks at the telephone call
Who is this dustbin?
This home for a clock and a key?
It's my dog, Fidget.

Rhys Siddons (9)
Pasture Primary School, Goole

The Journey To The Sea

As the adventure begins through the middle of Wales,
The rain falls on the mountains and then makes a boggy pool,
Oozing with dribbles and tricklings looking like a soggy bog.
Bad luck for him, he has to go the long way to the sea.
220 miles to where he wants to be.
All the streams flowing along with him.
Then he comes to a funny place that's called a v-shaped valley.
Then he comes to a tributary.
He likes it because he gets to meet old friends
When he joins with them.
'Oh no' now he's coming to the big waterfall.
Finally he is in the big pool at the bottom, the plunge pool.
He always carries earth and sand,
The river gets bigger all the time, so it gets better.
Now there's lots of sand
There's a very high tide now,
Now the tide's got even higher.
There's lots of high sandy and muddy banks
All around the water.
'Are we nearly there yet?' asks the river.
'Yes! Can you see the seaweed?' replies the wind.
It's rushing and roaring,
Finally he's there.

Jade Batty (10)
Pasture Primary School, Goole

My Cat

My cat is playful,
My cat is stripy,
He has a long tail,
My cat is soft,
His name is Mog,
He really hates dogs.

Rhys James (10)
Pasture Primary School, Goole

My Journey To The Sea

As I form in a boggy pool, I create a stream
Here on my journey to the sea
I dribble and trickle and rain drops on to me
As I make my journey to the sea.

I flow and flow
Suddenly a tributary joins on to me
So I say 'How are you?'
I start to roll downhill
I am diving into a plunge pool.
Finally that was over,
I make a v-shaped valley
I cut into the rocks
I am nearly there
Where am I going?
I am getting lower and lower
I made a flood plain,
I'm home, out to sea I go.

Rebecca Hardman (10)
Pasture Primary School, Goole

Friends

Friends are funny but sometimes not
Friends are silly but sometimes not
Friends are cool but sometimes not
Friends are wicked but sometimes not
Friends are expert but sometimes not
Friends are dudes but sometimes not.

Friends are good.

Matthew Graves (9)
Pasture Primary School, Goole

My Crazy School

In my school we have . . .
Hyenas in the hall,
Donkeys in the doorways,
Whales on the windows,
Dogs on the desks,
Bats on the white boards,
Slugs in the sports hall,
Owls in the office,
Bunnies in the bushes,
Crocodiles as calculators,
Flocks on the field,
Goats in the garden,
Tarantulas in the toilets
And worst of all our
Head teacher is a *horse!*
I think I've had enough of this crazy school.

Holly Wilkinson (9)
Pasture Primary School, Goole

Bullying

Bullying, bullying, bullying,
Happens every day,
Bullying, bullying, bullying,
Happens every way.
Bullying, bullying, bullying,
Makes everybody cry,
Bullying, bullying, bullying,
They lie, they lie, they lie.
    Don't be a
      bully!

Monica Ip (10)
Pasture Primary School, Goole

Cycling To Work

One morning cycling to work,
My grandma met an Alsation.

One morning cycling to work,
An Alsation bit her on the leg.

One morning cycling to work,
My grandma saw an Alsation.

One morning cycling to work,
An Alsation saw my grandma.

One morning cycling to work,
They put a bandage on her leg.

One morning cycling to work,
They took her to hospital.

After work one day,
My grandma's leg was infected.

Jake Lewis (9)
Pasture Primary School, Goole

Autumn's Here

Autumn is here and my branches are cold
All of my colours have blown away
The leaves were my crackly quilt
They all kept my body warm
But now the autumn breeze is here
And spring has blown away
What if the autumn breeze stays
And spring never comes back?
I do hope spring comes back again
Because I liked it then
When I was gold, green, brown and yellow
Standing tall in the sun.

Jamie Chilcott (10)
Priory Primary School, Hull

The Vampire's Night Out

All day he's asleep
Never dares to peep,
For the daylight
Is far too bright.

The night-time falls
When the night bird calls,
He walks round the town
The streets up and down.

Looking for a human,
There's a man by a van,
He crept from the back
About to attack!

But the man had some power
He drove off at 60 miles per hour,
The vampire just tutted,
For he was ever so gutted.

He started to wonder
Began to ponder,
He had a shave
Then went to his grave.

Jasmine Wright (10)
Snaith CP School, Snaith

Britain

Britain is cold
Britain is wet
And now I have met
A conker tree, a conker tree
That's bigger than me
I wonder who's got a conker tree
In their back garden, like me?
Pick down a conker, tie it with string
Play all night until morning begins.

Katie Oliver (10)
Snaith CP School, Snaith

Winter

Winter's a time for presents and surprises,
Playing in the snow and skidding on ice,
People enjoy Christmas Day,
With turkey and snowball delight.

Snowmen are made from sparkly snow,
And add on sticks and coal,
But please don't forget the carrot,
For a pointy nose.

Wrap up warmly when going out,
In hat and scarf and gloves,
You jump up and down and twirl around,
Making a lot of thumping sound.

Holly on different kinds of bushes,
Lovely mistletoe above to kiss,
Tickly tinsel to wrap around the tree,
Presents from Santa for you and me.

Christmas is lovely and bright,
What a pity Santa comes at night.

Heather King (9)
Snaith CP School, Snaith

My Family

My family is the best
There's me, my mum and all the rest
But sometimes I can be a pest
There's my dad
Careful, he can get mad
And that makes me get very sad.
Where's my mum?
Wow! A ring for my thumb
Look at her, she's drinking rum
Now there's me
I'm here for you to see
So this is my happy family.

Jessica Holmes (10)
Snaith CP School, Snaith

My Otter

My otter is the best
She stands out from the rest.

She stays in the water
And her last name is Porter.

She has got flat feet
And does not need a pot to eat.

She crunches at the fish bones
And knows when it is dinner time.

She likes her fish stale
And she is a female.

Her name is Nova
And lives near Dover.

My otter is the best
She just simply stands out from the rest!

Rebecca Watts (10)
Snaith CP School, Snaith

Autumn

Sun is down
It's dark in the town.

Apples in the tree
Only one I can see.

Lots of crispy leaves on the floor
If you're not careful they'll blow through your door.

Conkers falling,
Wind calling.

Leaves rich gold and brown
Like the jewels of a crown.

Summer, spring, autumn and winter.
Autumn's here, winter's near.

Georgina Gallagher (10)
Snaith CP School, Snaith

My Mum Loves Me!

My mum cooks for me,
My mum looks after me,
My mum loves me!

My mum kisses me,
My mum hugs me,
My mum loves me.

My mum makes my breakfast,
My mum makes my dinner,
My mum loves me!

My mum loves me lots and lots
My mum loves me!

Amy Brice (8)
Sutton Park Primary School, Kingston-upon-Hull

She Is . . .

She is . . .
My best friend
Good swimmer
Not bad at football

She is . . .
A good singer
Patient
Thoughtful

She does . . .
Goes to Bridlington
Listens to me
Cares for me!

Shannon Carr (10)
Sutton Park Primary School, Kingston-upon-Hull

Nature

Nature is so beautiful
It follows you wherever you go
In winter
The old trees splinter
As you dance by the bright moonlight
What a marvellous sight.

In summer as the fruit gets plumper
In the heat
There's no sleet
Flower buds break
But as a beautiful mistake.

In spring
As the bells go ding dong ding
And birds begin to sing
As the golden eagle spreads a wing
And a sparrow in a tree so narrow
Sings his little tune
From morning to noon
What a beautiful world.

Emma Smith (8)
Sutton Park Primary School, Kingston-upon-Hull

He Is . . .?

He is a funny boy
Who will turn into a crafty man
He is a pizza man
And can't open a can.

He is a horrible-looking man
Who one day turns into a Hull City fan.
But still can't open a can?
Because he isn't a Hull City fan!

James Mobbs (9)
Sutton Park Primary School, Kingston-upon-Hull

My Pet Rabbit Lucky

My pet rabbit Lucky
Can run super fast
If he ran around the world he wouldn't be last.

My pet rabbit Lucky
Likes his food
If you don't give him enough he gets in a mood.

My pet rabbit Lucky
Has very soft fur
If a cat saw him it would sit there and purr!

My pet rabbit Lucky
Can jump really high
In fact if he tried he could jump to the sky!

My pet rabbit Lucky
Is the best one of all,
He isn't too fat, he isn't too small and he certainly isn't too tall.

My pet rabbit Lucky,
Is the right one for me,
He is the perfect size, and as cute as can be!

Bethany Watson (9)
Sutton Park Primary School, Kingston-upon-Hull

My Grandma

G is for gardens which my grandma loves including the bugs
R is for reading which she shares with me
A is for arms for cuddles and hugs
N is for night-time in her bed I sleep you see
D is for dinner and my grandma's are the best
M is for music and she will sing along with the rest
A is for always I know she will always be there for me.

Sarah Sharpless (10)
Sutton Park Primary School, Kingston-upon-Hull

A To Z Of Monsters

A is for alligator - with a scary smile
B is for bogeyman - covered in bile
C is for cupboard - monsters hide there
D is for Dracula - got sharp teeth there
E is for Emily - my scary sister
F is for frightened - look at that mister
G is for Grim Reaper - with the sharp scythe
H is for horrible - he's got a knife
I is for ice man - covered in snow
J is for jellyman - scary I know
K is for killer who's on the loose
L is for lightning - quicker than a goose
M is for monster - horrible and slimy
N is for night - it's dark, cor blimey
O is for octopusy - who's got no head
P is for Peter - he should be dead
Q is for Queecho - who makes noises at night
R is for Romans - with gladiator fights
S is for Shadowman - who's real name is Mangs
T is for tarantula - with sharp fangs
U is for underwood - the origin of monsters
V is for Velo - eating some flonsters
W is for winner - the scariest one
X is for Xono - training his pet mon
Y is for yamihami - talking to take
Z is for zombie - my best mate.

Ian Parr (9)
Sutton Park Primary School, Kingston-upon-Hull

What Is A Million?

(In the style of Wes Magee)

The strange green aliens out in space
All the stars having a race
Since you were born, all the people you've seen
Every time you've made the car clean
All the time the world went round
All the people who have spent a pound
All the computers that have never switched on
All the planes that have dropped a bomb
All the times you have slammed the door
All the people who are really poor
All the friends you have had
Every time you have been mad
All the times you have been helped
All the otters that have slept in Kelp
All the names people have got
All the potters that have made a pot
That's sixteen million.

Jeff Humphrey (10)
Sutton Park Primary School, Kingston-upon-Hull

I Love The Taste Of Sizzling Sausages

I love the taste of sizzling sausages
plunked in a pan,
But I don't like the burnt ones
They always taste so strong,
In my tummy is where they belong.

I love the taste of sizzling sausages
plunked in a pan
I just love sausages
They are yummy, yum-yum.

Amy Mumby (8)
Sutton Park Primary School, Kingston-upon-Hull

A Horse For Love

As the sun rose over hilltops
And the mist lifted off the ground
A herd of ponies grazing
Stirred at the slightest sound.

A flock of birds flow overhead
Their leader cried out aloud
A mare and foal were worried
And they fled across the ground.

The herd's leader was a mighty horse
His neck was thick and strong
His powerful legs, they give him speed
He gathered his mighty throng.

Laura Andrew (8)
Sutton Park Primary School, Kingston-upon-Hull

Swimming Pool

S wimming is the best
W e are going swimming
 I love swimming
M y mates are very good at swimming
M y armbands help me
 I am in the top group
N ow it's time to go
G oing, going, gone.

P ools are fun
O h no I'm drenched
O h, I don't want to go home
L ovely, lovely pools.

Lauren Spenceley (8)
Sutton Park Primary School, Kingston-upon-Hull

I Didn't Get One Of Those!

'Hey you for Christmas I got an Xbox,'
'I didn't get one of those.'
'I got a Gamecube,'
'I didn't get one of those.'
'I got a slide,'
'I didn't get one of those.'
'I got a skateboard,'
'I didn't get one of those.'
I got a CD player,'
'I didn't get one of those.'
'I got a climbing frame,'
'I didn't get one of those.'
'I got a DVD player,'
'I didn't get one of those.'
'I got a half-pipe,'
'I didn't get one of those!'
'I got a real wrestler,'
'I didn't get one of those!'
'I got a private jet,'
'What! I definitely did not get one of those!
But I did get a new friend.'

Ashley Edmonds (9)
Sutton Park Primary School, Kingston-upon-Hull

My Mum

My mum looks as blue as the sea
My mum sounds like green wildlife
She feels like summer
She tastes like burger and chips
My mum is as precious as everything
My mum is special because she is mine.

Kieron Wegg (8)
Sutton Park Primary School, Kingston-upon-Hull

My Best Friend

My best friend looks like an amethyst
As it is as beautiful as my family
She sounds like silver when it shines like a medal.
She feels like summer when I can splash in the pool.
She tastes as good as spaghetti.
My best friend is as precious to me as my teddy.
She is special because she is my very own.

Kerry Baxter (7)
Sutton Park Primary School, Kingston-upon-Hull

Paddy

Paddy looks like as it stands for my birthday
Paddy sounds like the colour of gold.
Paddy feels like because I swim
He tastes as good as a burger.
Paddy is as precious to me as a football.
Paddy is special because he is mine.

James Piercy (7)
Sutton Park Primary School, Kingston-upon-Hull

My Mum

My mum helps me play the game
My mum looks like a ruby as it glows deep red
She feels like a comfy bear
She tastes as good as a Coke drink
My mum is precious to me
My mum is so special to me.

Adam Herbert (7)
Sutton Park Primary School, Kingston-upon-Hull

What Is A Million?

(In the style of Wes Magee)

The number of fingers on the windowpane
All the bullets shot in a world war in vain
The tears cried and dropped like rain
The number of people who crawled on a train
The hopes people wished for
The number of people who step out the door
Footprints of centuries on the floor
That's a million.

Emily Sparne (9)
Sutton Park Primary School, Kingston-upon-Hull

Kerry

My best friend looks like an amethyst when it sparkles at me.
She sounds like purple when it reminds me of violets.
She feels like when I go out in the garden.
She tastes as good as ice cream.
She is as special to me as a teddy.
My friend is special to me because she is mine.

Laura Jackson (7)
Sutton Park Primary School, Kingston-upon-Hull

My Mum

My mum looks like a pearl
My mum sounds like a lilac
She feels like a summery day
She tastes as good as chocolate cake
My mum is as precious to me as my dad
My mum is special because she is all mine.

Claire Hambly (7)
Sutton Park Primary School, Kingston-upon-Hull

My Sister

My sister looks like a diamond as she sparkles at me.
My sister looks like a sunset.
She feels like summer and looks like a bee.
She tastes as good as some burgers and some chips
And some chicken.
My sister is precious to me as she plays with me.
My sister is special to me because she is all mine.

Ria Richardson (7)
Sutton Park Primary School, Kingston-upon-Hull

My Sister

My sister looks like a diamond
My sister sounds like red
She feels like snow in December
And she tastes as good as pizza and chips.
My sister is so precious to me as a teddy
My sister is special to me because she is mine.

Danielle Bellamy (7)
Sutton Park Primary School, Kingston-upon-Hull

James' Pie

James looks like a diamond as it shines so bright
James' pie sounds like gold as Hull City.
He tastes better than burger and chips.
My rabbit is precious to me.
My friend James is special to me
Because he's there.

Patrick Langdale (7)
Sutton Park Primary School, Kingston-upon-Hull

Lions

Majestic lions are the king of all beasts,
They rule the jungle from west to east,
They stride along the open plains,
With their heads held high and feral manes.

Lazy lions sleep all day
While the lionesses hunt their prey,
She creeps and crawls and then she'll pause,
Then pounce and kill with teeth and claws.

At the food they'll rip and tear,
But the king will take the lion's share,
To regal sleep now, he's fed,
For it's getting dark and it's time for bed.

Amy Aistrop (9)
Sutton Park Primary School, Kingston-upon-Hull

My Mum

My mum looks like a sparkling diamond
She sounds like orange like my best football
She feels like winter when I like to play with snowmen
She feels as good as McDonalds
She is as precious to me as my hamster,
My mum is special because she is mine.

James Pinder (8)
Sutton Park Primary School, Kingston-upon-Hull

My Friend

My friend looks like a diamond in the sky.
My friend sounds like the sun.
He feels like winter when I can build a snowman.
He tastes as good as spaghetti on a plate.
My friend is special to me because he is mine.

Jasmin Russell (7)
Sutton Park Primary School, Kingston-upon-Hull

A Week Of School

Saturday is fun
Sunday play on my game
Monday it's time to go to school
Tuesday is literacy
Wednesday is numeracy
Thursday come home
Friday it's time to say goodbye to your teacher.

Joshua Ffoulkes (8)
Sutton Park Primary School, Kingston-upon-Hull

My Friend

My friend is like a diamond
My friend's face shines in the sea
My friend's clothes are like winter
My friend tastes like chips
My friend sounds like a heart beating
My friend is the best because he's mine.

Justin Phillips (7)
Sutton Park Primary School, Kingston-upon-Hull

All About My Mum

My mum looks like a diamond
My mum sounds like shiny yellow
She feels like warm summer
She tastes as good as beef in gravy
My mum is as precious to me as Nanna
My mum is special because she is mine.

Sophie Edwards (8)
Sutton Park Primary School, Kingston-upon-Hull

Teachers

What do teachers do after school?
Do they go around acting like they are cool?
Do they act like teenagers?
Do they eat fast food?
Do they have their hair cut at the hairdresser's?
        Or
Do they act all old and boring at home
as they do at school?
Do they eat boring old vegetables all the time?
Do they wear old people's clothes?
Do they cut their own hair or go to a hairdresser's?

        Do they not act cool outside of school?
I will never know
        Will you?

Paige Denton (11)
Sutton Park Primary School, Kingston-upon-Hull

Month Poem

January is cold and wet
February is still cold and wet but the sun shines
March some sunny days
April go to some parties
May it's cold but not wet
June summer starts and hot days
July still very sunny
August very hot days and people go to the beach
September a cold autumn starts
October people are starting to dress up for Hallowe'en
November the 5th of November is Bonfire Night.
December we get presents because it is Christmas.

Chelsey Dixon (8)
Sutton Park Primary School, Kingston-upon-Hull

Life In The Pet Shop

One little puppy feeling sad
Two little kittens playing mad
Three sticklebacks swimming in the bowl
Four little ants slipping down the hole
Five parrots talking to each other
Six baby hamsters going to their mother
Seven guinea pigs sleeping in the hay
Eight baby gerbils that were just born in May
Nine rabbits nibbling away
Ten budgies on special offer today!

Caleb Higgins (9)
Sutton Park Primary School, Kingston-upon-Hull

Play Cinquain

Coming
To play with me
It's a fun time to play
I like to play with my best friend
Bye friend.

Liam Senior (9)
Sutton Park Primary School, Kingston-upon-Hull

Monkey Haiku

I saw a monkey
The monkey was super fast
That it ran away.

Luke Watkinson (8)
Sutton Park Primary School, Kingston-upon-Hull

My Favourite Thing

My favourite thing is . . .
You'll have to guess,
I'm not going to tell you,
You'll have to guess,
Is it hard?
Alright, I'll give you a clue,
It begins with C,
And it ends in E.
Now can you guess?
I knew you couldn't,
I thought it was easy,
But maybe not for you.
Alright I'll tell you now,
It is chocolate.

Charlotte Morgan (10)
Sutton Park Primary School, Kingston-upon-Hull

Cats And Dogs Haiku

Jumping on the fence
The cat did it quietly
The dog was asleep.

The dog was barking
The dog was barking loudly
To see the puppy.

The dog saw the cat
The dog rushed after the cat
The dog got the cat.

**Dale Dermott, Christopher Harding, Michael Seaman,
Aiden Tidswell, Steven Bolton, & Ashley Hatton-Brown (9)**
Sutton Park Primary School, Kingston-upon-Hull

The Week At School

Monday is boring
Tuesday is very silly
Wednesday is okay
Thursday is cool
Friday is weird
Saturday is fun
Sunday Hull FC plays
Before the week begins gain.

Dale Hickingbotham (9)
Sutton Park Primary School, Kingston-upon-Hull

Moon

With his many shapes
The moon is a secret agent.

He is the dad of all stars
And king of the sky.

The moon is wise and friendly
To kid stars and adults stars alike.

He has been through wars
And heard the dinosaurs roar!

He first met Neil Armstrong
That's why the planets are jealous of him.

The moon is like a big clock
With its power over the Earth.

Because the moon has lived so long
He is a facial landmark.

I look at him in awe
As he gently returns my stare.

Adam Green (10)
Thorpepark Primary School, Hull

Thunder

You feel invading darkness
Your personality slips away
As death comes taking ours
It departs.

You feel electrifying
As it shows.
You feel cold as the Arctic ocean
A creature drifting over you
As you leave.

The discordant thunder crashes
Sounding in your eyes and ears
You feel discontented, uncomfortable,
Isolated
Alone.

Ryan Westerdale-Price & Natasha Harding (10)
Thorpepark Primary School, Hull

Dolphins

Dolphins swim like the ocean itself
Lapping like a wave on the shore,
As blue as the sky,
As fast as a bird can fly.

Dolphins are as smooth as a baby's bottom
They like to live clean.
Bathing in the sea.
Their eyes are as big as a tennis ball
Looking at you wisely.
Dolphins swim in a skool like ours,
And play together like friends of ours.

Casey Watson (10)
Thorpepark Primary School, Hull

Log Fire

Log fire, log fire,
Burns brightly in the night
It's like a saviour from the darkness evil walls
It seems so scary if it falls
Now the logs are black
There's no escape from the fiery track
Is it hotter than a poker?
Yes it is, I'm not a joker!

Log fire, log fire,
Only thing to keep you warm
Warmer than a baby just born
A scrawny owl flies past
The wind blows it out
Now you try to scream and shout
It gets darker and darker
Now it's black
You're on your own
Scared as Hell
As the Reaper rings his bell.

Aaron Simpson (9)
Thorpepark Primary School, Hull

Tiger

Orange fur like an orange
Black strips as the midnight sky
When it's dawn he puts furry paws on the floor
Catches swift fleeing prey.

Antelope as tasty as chicken
Eats quickly like a pig
Tiger sleeps like a baby
Until he hunts again.

Rebecca Turton (9)
Thorpepark Primary School, Hull

The Sea . . .

As blue as the sky, too tired to lie,
As quilted as a cloud not touching the ground,
A long piece of land just like a big band,
Lays there all day long.

A big bit of water swirling and whirling,
Lots and lots of animals caring and wading.

As comfy as a bed, as soft as wool but strong like a bull,
Because sometimes it gets rough and rough and rough.

You wouldn't like it when it's rough,
Because it's really, really tough.
It's just like a puff of smoke and rope,
It just gets out of control.

But when it is calm it does no harm
Just watch you're careful
Don't be too dareful.

Carl Robinson (10)
Thorpepark Primary School, Hull

Our Classroom

Our classroom is like a hall
Our classroom is as big as an elephant
Our classroom is as big as a hat,
Our classroom is like a noisy room
Our classroom is like a barking dog
Our classroom is an office
Our classroom is like a loving class
Our classroom is the best class in the whole universe
Our classroom is a caring class and also has the
Best teacher and LSA in the world.
Our class is a herd of animals.

Jessica Rayner (10)
Thorpepark Primary School, Hull

Sea

It's swimming on the gritty sand
Lapping above the sea animals,
Looking as blue as the wintry sky,
Flowing like a boat,
It's very dull like a wall,
It swims like a dolphin itself,
Looking like a big soft blueberry,
The sea is like a large, swimming pool,
The waves are a big waterfall,
Like a big blue carpet.

F
  A
    L
      L
        I
          N
            G
              D
                O
                  W
                    N

David Harrison (10)
Thorpepark Primary School, Hull

SATs

SATs are a nightmare
They give me a fright
SATs are hideous
I can't sleep at night
SATs are boring
They make me go dizzy
My knees begin to tremble
And my blood goes fizzy.

Amanda Marquis (10)
Thorpepark Primary School, Hull

Lightning

I wish I could be lightning
I'd soar across the sky,
I wish I could be lightning
I don't know why.

Stabbing the ground
Stinging like nettles
That's what lightning's like.

Lightning is like fireworks
Flashing through the sky
Feeling its way like a nervous bird,
Hovering like a balloon.

It's as brief as a kiss or a hit and run,
Ruining every flower
Spoiling every beast
Crashing through the clouds, ruthlessly
Mercilessly and
Cruel.

Rebecca Lang (9)
Thorpepark Primary School, Hull

Snow

See the snow drifting and twirling
Through the icy night,
See it cover the world like a blanket
It's like a sparkle of light.

See the snow covering the world
It's like blocks of ice
See it hovering like a bird
Fluffy candy you can eat.

Snow is like diamonds
Twinkling from the clouds
It's like angels are descending
Through the winter's night.

Michael Stark (10)
Thorpepark Primary School, Hull

Christmas Tree

A Christmas tree is bright,
A Christmas tree has a light,
Christmas tree, Christmas tree, Christmas tree.

A Christmas tree looks like a bush,
A Christmas tree looks like a toothbrush,
Christmas tree, Christmas tree, Christmas tree.

An artificial tree is beautiful
An artificial tree is colourful
Artificial tree, artificial tree, artificial tree.

An artificial tree is like a snowflake,
An artificial tree is like a mosaic
Artificial tree, artificial tree, artificial tree.

A Christmas tree is white,
An artificial tree is usual,
A Christmas tree is like a slush,
An artificial tree is like a snake,
Christmas tree, artificial tree, Christmas tree, artificial tree.

Ryan Malton (10)
Thorpepark Primary School, Hull

Fog

Covers the sky,
Fills the world,
Puffs of smoke,
Curling round buildings and trees
Like a big ocean
Spreading round and round
Drowning the world as
It goes
Like wind so cold and frosty
Wraps the cities like a big quilt
Dancing in my dreams
Tops the world like cream.

Kelsea Scoins (9)
Thorpepark Primary School, Hull

Hailstones

As it drops from the sky
I look at its shape
As shiny as a diamond
As hard as a rock
Now that's what I call hailstones.

As cool as ice,
Sharp as a knife,
That's what I call hailstones.
So different from rain
As different as its colour
That is blue
As people say
That's what I call hailstones.

Definitely
Splash!
Crash!
As hailstones hit the ground
Smash!
It shatters into a thousand pieces
Silver is its colour
Its shapes are all different
Splash!
Crash!
Smash!
Now that's what I call hailstones!

Demi Hodgins (10)
Thorpepark Primary School, Hull

Stars

As white as snow,
As white as a sheep,
Sometimes I wish we could meet.

As solid as the moon,
As solid as the rocks,
But still sometimes I wish we could meet.

As solid as a cave,
As solid as cliffs as well,
I think shooting ones are the best.

Shooting through the sky,
Shooting through the moon,
Shooting through space,
Sometimes I wish I could shoot with it.

When it's snowing in the night, I look up and see the stars,
Like snowflakes and ice cubes in one way,
In the dark the stars are bright,
Still I wish we could meet and shoot through the sky,
I don't know why.

Daniel Jones (9)
Thorpepark Primary School, Hull

Snow

As white as a mouse
Snow is like an ice cube
As white as some sugar
Grainy and salt.
Snow is like a freezer
Colder inside
As white as plain paper
Spread over the Earth.

Nathan Schofield (10)
Thorpepark Primary School, Hull

Our Classroom

Our classroom is like a living room
With a family inside
Our classroom is as important as a kettle boiling,
Steamy like a hot bath or
As cold as ice.
Filled with opposites,
Naughty and nice.

Busy as a shopping trolley,
Packets full of Allsorts,
Tidy as my bedroom,
Organised of course!
Kids noisy as a walkie-talkie
Teachers noisy too!
Busy, busy working hard -
Lots of stuff to do.

Nicola Pilkington (10)
Thorpepark Primary School, Hull

Snow

I wish I could be snow
And drop on people sneakily
Ice down their backs
To chill to the bone.

White as a ruler
But softer than sawdust,
Sprinkling the world,
Like icing on a cake.

Cold as a refrigerator
Freezing everything,
Covering my house,
Like a white blanket.

Kade Cooke (9)
Thorpepark Primary School, Hull

Don't Forget

Underline your title dear
Underline the date
Draw in your margin dear
And don't be late!

Capital letters at the beginning dear
Full stops at the end
Don't forget to write in paragraphs dear
It drives me round the bend.

No spelling mistakes dear
No scribbles in your book
Now listen dear
Take your book and have a look.

Just remember dear
Only ten weeks till SATs
Revise, revise, revise dear
Then you'll have time to relax.

Tammy Milner & Charlotte Rowan (10)
Thorpepark Primary School, Hull

Snow

Cold as raindrops,
They fall upon the light blue sky,
Frozen like the inside of a freezer,
Feels like a soft sponge.

Snowmen made in the cold weather
Looks like a big white carpet over the world,
Lovely to watch it slowly coming down,
Good to play with.

Smells like blueberries
White as a cover bed spread over the world
Tastes the water, very slip down your throat.

Kristina Green (9)
Thorpepark Primary School, Hull

Fog

Grey as a mouse
Cold like ice
As damp as water
Spreading out.

Stinky as a sock
Freezing as snow
A dark cloud
Covering me.

Illuminating fog
Changes all,
Dragon's fire
Puffing smoke.

Dull as an attic
Dangerous sharp knife
Be careful
It's dangerous.

Bradley Franklin (9)
Thorpepark Primary School, Hull

Log Fire

As hot as the sun
As bright as a light
As big as an elephant
As red as a felt tip
As yellow as a banana
As orange as an orange
As much wood as a forest
As many flames as a thousand lighters
Burning bright.

Jamie Nolan (9)
Thorpepark Primary School, Hull

Christmas Tree

Christmas tree
Christmas tree
You are an amazing star
You shine like the sun
Keeping me warm and snugly in the soft
Winter's wind
Covering this house with a quilt.

You are as spiky as a hedgehog
You keep me safe through the night
Guarding my home
With bright green light.

Branches dressed with tinsel and lights
Beautiful tree stands there in our room.

Laura Chaffer (9)
Thorpepark Primary School, Hull

Fog

Fog is blurry
It's not very clear
I can't see, can you?

Fog is like a drowned face that
Is in front of you, saying things spookily,
Pitch-white no one can see
They only see in front
Never behind
Watch your back.

Fog wakes you with frosty fingers,
Making you freeze so you can't talk.

You can see your breath shivering
As it drifts off into the mist,
And slowly fades away.

Georgina Drewery (9)
Thorpepark Primary School, Hull

A Book

A book gives you quiet time to explore and be creative
It's a place you'll love to live,
All your dreams seem to be true.

If you treat it like a home,
You'll never be alone,
Surrounded by characters,
Warm and content.

Delicate as glass,
Precious as a family,
Rewarding as a prize,
Get yourself inside.

Break a book your heart will break too,
It's an object you can't repair - so beware!

Books should last a lifetime,
Books are as bright as the sun,
A book is worth every penny,
So handle with ease.

Sarah Mellors (10)
Thorpepark Primary School, Hull

Christmas Tree

Beautiful as a bauble,
Straight as an arrow,
Branches spread wide,
Green like a pepper,
Shining like the sun,
Green forest, stars shine above.
Angel looks down gently,
Watching lights and baubles.

Ashley Fox (9)
Thorpepark Primary School, Hull

Our Classroom

Our classroom is like a living room,
With a family squeezed inside,
Door as big as an elephant,
Square windows frame the world.
Whiteboard blank as snow,
Round clock counting the day,
Pupils noisy as a parrot,
Chattering away.

Jarrod Nicholson (10)
Thorpepark Primary School, Hull

Snow

As white as paper
Cool as an ice cube
Creeps over the ground
Like Jack Frost.

Snow is a cold friend,
Like a freezer inside,
White sugar sprinkled
Over land.

Tony Clark (9)
Thorpepark Primary School, Hull

Log Fire

Log fire is like a fire burning
Log fire is like a sky sunset
Log fire is like an orange car racing
Log fire is like a bright light shining
Log fire is like a kettle boiling
Log fire is like people walking
Log fire is like a huge candle.

David Benford (10)
Thorpepark Primary School, Hull

Snow

The snow is as cold as ice cubes
As white as a light
As hard as a brick
As slidy as an ice arena
As chilling as a freezer
Deep inside
Light as a flake of light
That's shining as it falls,
A freezing feather.

Josh Nichols (9)
Thorpepark Primary School, Hull

Ant

Scuttles like a bug,
Stings like a bee,
Blind like a dog,
Eats like a human,
Poisoned like a dead worm,
Jumps like a frog,
So small he can scurry through cracks
In the pavement,
Retreating to his own little world.

Ryan Thomas (9)
Thorpepark Primary School, Hull

Ants

Strong as a rock
Tight fisted like thunder
His eyes light as birds
He's as brave as a first kiss
Legs marching like soldiers on parade
An ant crawls by.

Nicky Robinson (10)
Thorpepark Primary School, Hull

FA Cup Final

It's time for kick-off
The time has finally come
The FA Cup final
The tension is high for Man U vs Arsenal.
The ref blows his whistle
Roy Keane's straight on the ball
He passes to Forlan
What a fantastic pass.
He shoots at goal
But the goalie pulls off a magical save.
Giggs to take the corner
It swerves to Ronaldo
But it rattles the woodwork
So close.
Now it's Arsenal's turn,
Ljungberg to Henry
Ferdinand tackles - a penalty
Henry to take it
In a flash it's 1-0.
Man U earns a free kick
Giggs to take it
Goal! 1-1
Ruud Van Nistelrooy on the ball
He shoots
'Goal!
As just before you know it, it's full-time
Man U wins!

Jack Humphries (9)
Tilbury Primary School, Hull

Volcanoes

A slight rumble shakes the island
People starting to stare
It's starting to smoke
It's dark and deadly
With a bright red glow
Lava dribbling down
It's ready to blow
And there's a big blast
There's a violent rumble
It's about to blow.
Oh no!

Jake Jones (9)
Tilbury Primary School, Hull

The Beautiful Stream

As I walked by the fast flowing stream.
I noticed how beautiful it was.
The fish were jumping.
The water was splashing.
The sun was shining.
The rocks were clashing.
And all was a beautiful day.

Ellie Dale (9)
Tilbury Primary School, Hull

Whizz

W hizzing and flying high in the sky
H urrying and scurrying past the parrots and clouds
I n and out of dark scary twisters
Z ooming and shooting just missing a king vulture
Z ooming home to have his supper.

Robbie Gillyon (9)
Tilbury Primary School, Hull

My Noisy Sister

When I went to bed
I felt a dread
I heard a noise, it was getting closer
It sounded like a cup and saucer.

My door was creaking
I was freaking
My toys started to fall off my wall
I felt very small.

I heard a voice
It sounded strange, but I made the choice
To go and see
What was frightening me.

It was only my sister
Sleepwalking with a blister
It was making her yelp
She needed some help.

So I got out bed
To help her and said
'Go back to bed
Your noise is hurting my head!'

Joshua Beavers (10)
Tilbury Primary School, Hull

Hull Fair

Hull fair, Hull fair
Watch the children stand and stare
Mouths wide eyes bright
Looking at the glorious sight.
Roundabouts go round and round
Listen to the wonderful sound.
Coconut shy candyfloss
Loads to eat for a treat.
Hull fair, Hull fair
Watch the children stand and stare.

Laura Smith (9)
Tilbury Primary School, Hull

My Little Life At Dancing

When I dance I spin and win exams
I wear a nice dress better than the rest
Some say I am magnificent, some don't even recognise me.
But I am a little bit nervous at the start.
My dance teacher says 'you need to get better'
But the next day I get a letter
I opened it just like a normal person would do,
And guess what it said 'Please can you do ten exams.'
My mum said 'Don't look at me, you decide yourself.'
I thought, thought and thought
It was on my mind all day
Some of my neighbours said
'Have you thought what you are going to do yet?'
I just say 'Go away please.'
All my life I've been waiting for this
So I said 'Yes' because someone gave it a miss.
I got to wear a top, pink and glittery
And a skirt to match
And guess what I won 1st prize.

Amber Humphries (10)
Tilbury Primary School, Hull

The King Cobra

The cobra slithers like a snail
When it's going for his prey
He strikes like a gun firing bullets
The cobra is big and cunning
When it bites it's a stunning sight
And doesn't leave without a fight.

Callum Stone (9)
Tilbury Primary School, Hull

The Axe

Drip and dribble, haunted house,
Full of bats and beetles and mice
An alarming sight
Terrified me as I stopped in fright,
Cobwebbed and creepy,
I enter, I scream!
A hovering axe, coming towards me!
I stooped down quickly, the axe hit the wall,
I wished so hard for it to be a dream.
Too bad, it's not.
I run and scurry, and flee from the mansion
Never will I enter again.

I turn,
Weeds all over,
The axe has stopped,
It has seen me
Oh no!
My long fair hair falls to the ground
I run and run and run . . .
Finally I see the sun.
No more walks for me!

Danielle Sowersby (10)
Tilbury Primary School, Hull

Waterfall

W hizzing, whirling
A t the top of the waterfall
T oday it will
E nd
R oaring across the seas, even the best one of them all
F lowing slowly, swiftly falling, slowing down
A nd
L isten to the call, oh you need to
L isten to the call, it's ssshhh falling down the waterfall.

David Benn (10)
Tilbury Primary School, Hull

The Special Football Match

One day it was sunny outside the perfect day
For the special match England vs Brazil
I was so excited.

The time was getting nearer to kick-off
The excitement was getting unbearable
Then it was time for kick-off
The whistle blew.

The action was amazing
The sight incredible
Beckham shoots at goal
He scores! Beckham for England
The end whistle blows
The score still 1-0.
The excitement starts to fade
We start to sleep and dream about the most
Fantastic game ever.

Vincent Brooks (10)
Tilbury Primary School, Hull

The Slow River

The slow river, winding round and round
Fish swimming all slippery and wet
A big brown bear stands waiting for
The fish to jump out
Ready to pounce
Gotcha!
The river continues
Meandering downstream
Trickling and creeping
Over rocks
White water goes round
Threading and winding
Roaming and crawling
The slow river winding round and round.

Andrew Benn (10)
Tilbury Primary School, Hull

A Dream Match

First half
Out come Hull
All the crowd are going barmy
Only boos and jeers from a north stand.

We've kicked off Hull vs Leeds
Colin Best is away down the wing
He is sprinting
But Calderwood has clung to Best
And has hauled him into touch
Leeds have the ball now
With McDonald he's broken through
And dived over an uncovered line
Sinfield to kick and gets an added 2 points
6-0 to Leeds.

Second half
Hull have kicked but it's a drop out
Swain has snatched a great kick
Offloads to Raynor and he's over the line
Cooke is saying his words
Great kick an extra two points for Hull
The crowd go potty.

Hull have the ball on the ten metre line
Swain goes for a drop goal
It's over!
Hull have won 7-6.

Ryan Lawler (10)
Tilbury Primary School, Hull

My Holiday

It's warm and sunny the best you could wish,
On the golden sandy beach with beautiful coloured fish
The cool shimmering swimming pool
That you could relax and swim in
Having fun, laughing and bathing,
Got a gorgeous tan that is just the best,
Better than at school having a maths test
Coming home in a few days
A bit down and sad,
Rather stay here with the sun than
Go home to mucky lads.
Have you guessed where the beautiful place is
Where I am?
Of course I'm at
      Cyprus!

Abigail Ellis (9)
Tilbury Primary School, Hull

Underneath The Ocean

I went underneath the ocean exploring
I saw something
I did not swim closer because it was moving
It was digging a hole
I was determined to know what it was doing
When I had waited for an hour and a half
I went over to see what it was
I looked down the hole
It had tunnelled deep
I didn't touch it for I didn't know if it was a home
I looked at my waterproof watch it was 10pm
I swam home waiting for the next day to begin.

Christina Smith (10)
Tilbury Primary School, Hull

February

F is for fishing which is lots of fun
E is for energy to help us run
B is for brains to help us think
R is for reindeer which have big horns
U is for unicorn which has a bright white coat
A is for art where you splish and splash
R is for raspberries they are purply
Y is for yellow which bananas are.

S is for snails which slither and slide
E is for eagles which screech and fly
A is for autumn which has brown crispy leaves
S is for snowflakes which sparkle and shine
O is for orange which you peel then eat
N is for numbers where you count up and down.

Jasmine Chilvers (9)
Tilbury Primary School, Hull

Walking With My Dad

When I walk my feet hurt so much
When I walk with Dad
I have to sit down for a minute
When I walk with Dad.
He has to pick me up sometimes
When I walk with Dad.
I really walk slowly when my feet are tired
When I walk with Dad.
I have to go on a ramble
When I walk with Dad.
Dad walks too fast
I have to run to keep up with him.

Sophie Langley (10)
Tilbury Primary School, Hull

On One Snowy Day

On one snowy day when the weather picks up a chill
When you pick up a handful of snow and throw it at
your friends, it flutters on the ground.
When you take another step the crunchy ice crunches
underneath your feet.
When you make snowmen, snowballs and snowangels
They melt and disappear.
Slippery ice on the ground underneath it makes a crunchy sound.
Rosy-red cheeks, freezing lips and cold fingertips.
When the snow turns to slush, it's all wet and soggy,
Snowflakes twirling around and around then onto the ground.

Jarrad Grainger (9)
Tilbury Primary School, Hull

What A Lovely Day

'What a lovely day' my mum would say
As the bright green grass blows in the breeze.

'What an amazing day' my nan would say
As the birds are singing sweetly in the trees.

'What an enjoyable day' my gran would say
As the snow-white clouds cover the rich blue sea.

'What a fine day' my aunt would say
As the excited people rush through the crowds.

'What a magnificent day' I would say
As the day turns into night.

Shannen Smith (9)
Tilbury Primary School, Hull

The Ice-Cold River

Is it cold? Is it frozen?
The ice-cold river glimmering in the sunlight.
Shall we go? Shall we not?
So I crept across the sparkling river
Will the coldness make me shiver?

Yes it does, my teeth chatter
As the waves clatter
My feet are freezing
As the wind starts breezing
So I go back home to the warm.

Jack Sullivan (9)
Tilbury Primary School, Hull

Boom, Bang, Bang!

People drinking beer and wine.
When the boom! it scares
The bang, terrified.
You see a sparkle
You see a twinkle
The amazing colourful fireworks go
Then the big one lets rip a roar
What a beautiful crimson gold.
The Catherine wheel is set
Blue, red, gold, silver and yellow it goes.
One in the ground sets off like a water fountain.

Liam Sawyers (9)
Tilbury Primary School, Hull

Rain

Rain clouds of grey bring the rain, rain,
Made of water droplets,
When the sun shines through they are like prisms.
I see a rainbow made from beautiful colours of . . .
Red,
Orange,
Yellow,
Green,
Blue,
Indigo,
Violet.

Sean Kemp (9)
Tilbury Primary School, Hull

Animals

Animals are all different sizes some small
Huge and enormous
Minute and miniature
Some are underground
And they make so little sound
Some are in the sky
Like birds flying so high
Some live in the water
And even have a daughter
Animals are all different sizes
That's no surprises.

Chelsea West (9)
Tilbury Primary School, Hull

The Football Match

At the football match
The crowd are shouting with excitement
When Liverpool kick-off
The crowd go wild
Then the whistle blows in half-time.
The score still 0-0.

Second half
Man united to start
The whistle blows the excitement builds up again
Michael Owen gets into the box
He's brought down by Giggs
Penalty.
The crowd go silent
Owen plays back
He kicks the ball
Goal!
The final whistle blows
Final score 1-0 to Liverpool.

Chantelle Dixon (10)
Tilbury Primary School, Hull

Sally

Sally is black and white
Short soft hair
Her nose is black and wet
Sally's tail wags very fast
It makes a cold draught.
She sleeps in the kitchen
In a plastic bed with a nice clean blanket
For her head.
Sally has a tub of water and a grey dog bowl.

Louis Burdett (10)
Tilbury Primary School, Hull

I Wonder

I wonder what it's like on Mars?
Are there aliens eating chocolate bars?
And space rockets going zooming by,
I hope if I go I'll be able to fly.

I wonder what it's like in Heaven?
I suppose it's a bit like the county of Devon.
Will I be able to sunbathe in a white fluffy cloud
Or I could go shopping without there being a crowd?

I wonder what it's like under the deep blue sea?
I want to meet a kind shark and get back in time for tea.
Will I meet some dolphins and swim with them all day?
Or I could ride with some unknown fish so beautiful and gay.

Katy Simpson (10)
Withernwick Primary School, Hull

Feelings

When I am lonely I feel as purple as a bruised plum
When I am happy I feel as orange as the rising sun
When I am sad I feel as brown as a dug up potato
When I am mad I feel as grey as a stormy cloud
When I am tired I feel as turquoise as the wide sparkling ocean
When I am angry I feel as black as the midnight sky
When I am frightened I feel as red as red grapes fresh from the vine
When I am tearful I feel as silver as the sparkling stars
When I am wishful I feel as white as fresh fallen snow
When I am excited I feel multicoloured!

Heather Croft (8)
Withernwick Primary School, Hull

I Wish, I Wish . . . I Wonder, I Wonder . . .

I wish I was a sky lark so I could sing sweetly all day
I wish I was a jump-jet pilot
I would fly to the Milky Way.
I wish I was a fish in the ocean
So I could search the deep blue sea.
I wish I was a kangaroo
I would jump so high for all the world to see.

I wonder, I wonder . . .

I wonder why the sun is yellow and bright
I wonder why the rainbow is beautiful and light
I wonder why the oceans have waves so big and strong
I wonder why the road to nowhere is always so long.

    I wish and I wonder . . .

William Rowley (11)
Withernwick Primary School, Hull

I Wish . . .

I wish I was a leopard running as fast as the speed of sound.
I wish I was a blue motorbike zooming down the road.
I wish I was a rich and famous popstar
I wish I was in outer space.

I wish I was snowdrifting down from the sky.
I wish I was rain splashing in the rivers.
I wish I was a star in the night sparkling and bright.
I wish that I was the sun that shone in the sky all day.
I wish I was a bird so I can fly in the sky so high.

    I wish . . . I wish . . . I wish . . .

Zoe Mitchell (10)
Withernwick Primary School, Hull

Who? What? Why? Where? When?

Who made God?
Who is the kindest man in the world?
Who made the most inventions?
Who?

What is in the deepest part of the sea?
What was it like in the Great War?
What is it like to be a secret agent?
What?

Why does the world spin?
Why is the universe endless?
Why is the Earth round?
Why?

Where do green UFOs come from?
Where is our Lego man?
Where does the rainbow end?
Where?

When will we meet slimy aliens?
When did our world begin?
When will time end?
When?

Daniel Walker (9)
Withernwick Primary School, Hull

The Land Animals

The snow dog sat like a statue on the mountain
The lion roars like an earthquake
The tiger ran after the deer like a F1 car
Racing on a track
The monkey ran up the tree like someone
Throwing a ball in the sky.

Craig Pitts (10)
Wold Primary School, Hull

The Magic Key

I have a key that opens the gates of Heaven
In that Heaven there is a twinkling star
In that twinkling star there is my dad
And in my dad there is a loving heart
And in that loving heart there is me
Because I love him.

I have a key that opens the door of a sunflower
In that sunflower there is a seed
In that seed there is a life
And in that life there is my dad
And in my dad there is a sun
And in that sun there is a smile
Which opens my heart.

Amy Kerman (11)
Wold Primary School, Hull

My Dream Box

When I can't get to sleep I open my box
And dream of the KC Stadium of Hull FC
Winning the super league.
Of me walking on the moon,
Being a rugby player for Hull FC
Living in Portugal.

I dream of breathing underwater
Of being a manager for Hull FC
Been in a never-ending Mexican wave
I dream of having an aviary full of parrots and cockatoos.

I dream of being a bird flying over mountains.

Louis Cook (9)
Wold Primary School, Hull

Hagrid's House

In the kitchen is . . .
An enormous old and dusty stove
A pewter tankard filled with frothy butterbeer
A crumpled recipe book for potions
A huge knife for cutting Fang's red, juicy meat
And the only sound is,
A humongous boiling kettle.

In the bedroom is . . .
An old rusty brown belt hanging over a chair
A colossal wooden, comfy bed,
A photo of Dumbledore in a rusty frame,
An old wardrobe filled with scruffy clothes,
And the only sound is,
The wind whistling through the window.

In the attic is . . .
A crack in the wall where the spiders crawl
A gang of bats flying around
A hat that has never been worn
And the only sound is,
The squeaking of the bats.

Gareth Mathie (8)
Wold Primary School, Hull

Springer Spaniel

A paw scratcher
A stick catcher
A play bouncer
A cat chaser
A slaver maker
A bone chewer
A dig drooler
A tail wagger.

Tessa Grimes (10)
Wold Primary School, Hull

Smarties

What does it taste like?
What does it sound like?
What does it look like?
What does it smell like?
What does it feel like?

It sounds like a steam train running on the track
It sounds like an egg frying in a pan spitting and boiling
It sounds like a rattlesnake getting very angry
It sounds like bacon sizzling in a pan.

It smells like brown potatoes fresh and ready to eat
It smells like red raspberries red as ever
It smells like hot rich golden chocolate.

It looks like a flying saucer spinning in space
It looks like a car wheel worn out and well used
It looks like an eye staring at you
It looks like the Earth being squashed to the South Pole.

It tastes like a crisp when you bite the shell
It tastes delicious when you take a bite
It tastes of golden luxury creamy chocolate.

It feels like a smooth slippery stone
It feels like a rough mountain on the inside
It feels like slippery, slimy mud squelching in your shoes.

Stephen Forton (10)
Wold Primary School, Hull

An Extreme Skate Park

An extreme place
Where people fly really high
Up amazing ramps
Grinding solid steel
As you feel freedom.

Ashley Hill (10)
Wold Primary School, Hull

Box Of Dreams

My box of dreams is deep, deep blue with glittering stars all around,
My box is smooth and round.

I love to dream about dancing in a show,
Sweet smelling flowers in a sunny meadow,
A shop full of cute teddies from top to bottom,
Monkeys swinging in a great big jungle,
Living in the delicious land of chocolate,
Swimming with the soft and lovely dolphins,
Sitting on top of the glittering moon,
Walking with the film stars,
Walking down a dusty road with a new dog,
Going shopping with my best friends.
Having a huge sparkling party all day long,
Having long, silky hair.

When I wake up I need to know
Which magical dreams are there.
So I open my box
To let the enchanted dreams fill the air!

Nikki Brown (9)
Wold Primary School, Hull

My Dreams

My box is glittery while it sparkle with joy
It is pink with a purple bow
My best dream ever would be to climb the highest mountain
My next dream would be to work in the deep to feed the tropical fish.
My next dream would be to have dinner with Avril Lavigne.
I would like to jump out the cold water with the dolphins.
My dream would be to treasure between my mum and dad for ever
My dream would be to be an actress in Casualty.

Stephanie Kinch (9)
Wold Primary School, Hull

Box Of Dreams

My box is rectangle in shape with black and white stripes,
with a Hull FC badge on top.

My box is full of dreams and dreams.

I dream of being a rugby player of running out onto the pitch
wearing my black and white strip.

Sometimes I dream of soaring the blue sunny skies
as the pilot of a jet plane.

I dream of holidays in Cornwall,
of long sunny days on the beach
playing in the sand with my family.

Sometimes I dream of a world where no animals
are hurt and can live happy and safe.

Jordan Eastwood (9)
Wold Primary School, Hull

My Dream Box

I have this light blue box that's sparkly all around
When I go to bed I open my box and let my dreams come out
I close my eyes and I start dreaming of my favourite things
I dream of swimming in the Olympic races and winning
I dream of having dinner with all the Hull FC players
I dream for Hull FC being top of the league
I dream of being really rich
I dream of me and my friends being pop stars doing tours.
I dream of being a mascot for Hull FC.
I dream of swimming with glamorous dolphins.

All my dreams are glamorous things
And when I awake I can't wait for the next night of dreams.
That's why my box of dreams is special.

Bethany Lowden (9)
Wold Primary School, Hull

The Bogeyman's House

In the cellar is . . .
A jar of children's eyeballs
A tub of human flesh
A bin of gooey liver
A jar of blood from animals
And the only sound is
Mice scurrying across the floor.

In the kitchen is . . .
A pan full of children's body parts
A big bottle of brains
A humungous pan of people ready to eat
A bony skeleton hung up on the wall
And the only sound is
A pan bubbling on the cooker.

In the bedroom is . . .
A big pair of pants
A disgusting floor with dust all over
A black cat with yellow eyes
A pile of clothes what are covered in dirt
And the only sound is:
The cat miaowing.

In the attic is . . .
An old spellbook
A wall full of pictures
An old rocking chair
A heap of crooked bones on the dusty floor
And the only sound is
The old rocking chair rocking.

Hannah Bromby (8)
Wold Primary School, Hull

My Box Of Dreams

My box is lilac and pink with glitter
With a big blue bow on top
I store all my very good dreams in it
When I cannot go to sleep
I close my eyes and think
Of swimming with a lovely dolphin
Being a professional ice skater
Getting a little spaniel or a cute kitten
Playing for a girls' football team on TV
Having lots of funny friends
Being a snow queen up in my sparkling castle
When I wake up in the morning
I just can't wait till the next night
Because my dreams are so exciting!

Laura Cawthra (9)
Wold Primary School, Hull

My Dream Box

My box is purple with yellow glitter
It is small and round
My box has a gold ribbon around it
And it gleams in my sleep.

I dream of being on a hot sandy beach
Sharing love with my family
Giving friendship to my friends
Sitting in a limo with Gareth Gates.

I dream of swimming in a blue ocean
Sitting on a rainbow
To catch a bright star
Going on holiday.

Lauren McNeil (9)
Wold Primary School, Hull

Hagrid's House

In the kitchen is . . .
An enormous old and dusty stove
A pewter tankard filled with frothy butterbeer
A crumpled recipe book for potions
A huge knife for cutting Fang's red juicy meat
And the only sound is . . .
An old humongous boiling tin kettle.

In the bedroom is . . .
An old rusty brown belt hanging over a chair
A colossal wooden and comfy bed
A photo of Dumbeldore in a shiny frame
An old wardrobe filled with scruffy robes
And the only sound is . . .
The wind whistling through windows.

In the attic is . . .
A crack in the wall where the spiders crawl
A pack of bats hanging on walls
A spider crawling in the corner
A bulky cloak hung up
And the only sound is . . .
Bats squeaking.

Reece Harvey (8)
Wold Primary School, Hull

My Favourite Box

My box is the colour of sunset
With sparkly ribbon.
The ribbon is purple with gold glitter
In my special box there is beautiful beads.
The sun is setting across the sky lovely piano music playing
While the waves splash against the rocks
Fish jump up and down
In my dreams there is my family
Having a party with loud music.

Sammie-Jay Hackett (9)
Wold Primary School, Hull

The Vampire's House

In the cellar . . .
A giant pot of blood,
A muddy black cape,
A pair of gooey teeth,
A pan of people
And the only sound is,
The old rocking chair creaking.

In the kitchen is . . .
A heap full of bones,
A tap that drips out fresh fangs,
A box of people's old flesh,
A corner of spiders
And the only sound is,
The tap dripping.

In the bedroom is . . .
A big black bat hanging from the cobweb ceiling,
A stained glass mirror,
A ragged rug,
A big crack in the ceiling,
And the only sound is,
The squeaking of the bats.

In the attic is . . .
A dusty coffin full of bones,
A humongous pair of shoes
A big dark corner
A broken rocking chair
And the only sound is,
People yelling for *help!*

Gemma Iveson (8)
Wold Primary School, Hull

The Good Fairy's House

In the cellar is . . .
a very nice place where someone lives
a broken wand
a small rubbery pair of shoes
a box with teeth in it
and the only sound is fluttering wings all around the room.

In the kitchen is . . .
a little pot full of food,
a tiny tap with twisty lids,
a little fridge full of cold drinks,
a box full of tiny forks,
and the only sound is rustling coats when they have been put on.

In the bedroom is . . .
a row of fifty small beds
a cupboard with their slippers in
a bag with bobbles in it
a set of games,
and the only sound is,
jumping on the beds.

In the attic is . . .
a box full of broken old family haircombs
a broken wand with snap and rules near it
a squashed basket
a beautiful dress with diamonds on it
and the only sound is,
the wind in the attic whistling through holes in the roof.

Darcey Black-Foy
Wold Primary School, Hull

Smarties

They sound like a pack of deadly rattlesnakes slithering across
the fiery-hot African desert.
They sound like a talented Spanish woman dancing around
shaking her brilliant colourful patterned castanets.

They look like hovering spaceships with brown men on a mission
to kill us
They look like round buttons on an old waistcoat or on a
king's mighty colourful robe.

They feel like walls and really hard things and a tortoiseshell
with its traveller underneath.
They feel smooth and hard like a cracked brick wall
the inside is mud squelching under your feet.

They smell like rich chocolate ice cream in your mouth and
beautiful oranges under your nose and in your mouth
the lovely scaly taste of the orange peel rubbing on your tongue.

They taste like beautiful Dairy Milk chocolate resting on your
tongue waiting to be chewed to bits.
It tastes like red strawberries waiting to be crushed by your teeth.

Sam Baker (10)
Wold Primary School, Hull

Under The Sea

Shells lying at the bottom of the ocean
like a village of houses.
A blow fish blowing up like a balloon floating in the air.
Jellyfish floating legs moving like a fork of noodles
being put on a plate
A glassfish tip toeing on the ocean waves like a person
trying to sneak out.
An eel wriggling into the sand like a chip being dipped in ketchup.
The aqua ocean sparkling like stars on a misty night.
All the fish and mammals are going to their dens and holes
like children going to sleep.
All quiet now. Sssssssshhhhhhh.

Jenna Stewart (10)
Wold Primary School, Hull

Box Of Dreams

My box is amber, black and made of wood . . .
My wish that they come true if only they could . . .
The wonderful things about having a dream is that you can
Be anything or so it would seem . . .
To score the goal and make the team win
To be top of the league, where shall I begin . . .
This year we will go on and go up to Division Two
A better chance of the cup . . .

With my silver boots and a steady nerve
Each ball I kick will watch it swerve into the net
again and again it will go
Who's the man of the match?
Everyone will know in dreams gone by.
Another year gone another season and promotion to Division One
The crowds cheer when they hear my name . . .
Every week they shout it's always the same
Beckham is bought, scores with a chip my dream.
Hull City in the premiership

Richard Clayphan (9)
Wold Primary School, Hull

Book Of Dreams

On my desk there is a book
It's shiny red and circular
It is a book full of dreams
I dream of Manchester United beating
Liverpool one-nil
Gentle snow as high as I am
Discovering an unknown sea
No more wars so peace and harmony
Playing for Man U and earning lots of money
My dad not working again
That school was not invented
The pleasure of scoring a goal at hockey
I rush upstairs to open my book and fall into dream Heaven.

Jamie Mosey (9)
Wold Primary School, Hull

My Box Of Dreams

My box of dreams is a football one with red, black and white
squares on it,
and in the box is a stormy beach smashing against the walls,
and a football stadium with players playing on the pitch
and birds flying around singing their beautiful songs,
a quad-bike jumping up and down while it's going up hills
and breath of a dragon warming up your hands,
a crowded cheering in the stadium for their teams
a dark misty night with stars shining as bright as the moon,
the dreams of me and my grandad having fun,
and a quiet beach flowing backwards and forward.
Watching football players scoring lots of goals,
the rain drizzling down from the dark clouds,
watching lighting striking down on your garage roof.
I dream of being a mascot for Hull City,
I dream of playing football with Hull City,
I would dream of getting all of the Hull City shirts and Liverpool's
and giving many to my friends.
If I am a football player I dream of getting trained by John Arna Rise.
I dream of all happy things.

Joe Marshall (10)
Wold Primary School, Hull

A Dream Come True

My box is purple with glitter all over the lid.
It glows in the dark with pink dazzling ribbon
The box is full of delighting dreams
My dream would be to go to Australia
and swim with dolphins.
In my other dream I would love to go to a water forest
and hear the birds tweeting and flying through trees
and water splashing all over the rocks.
I would like to go to the South Pole and groom the polar bears.
My dream would be to go and live in a mansion and
sit in a hot tub.

Emma Farnill (9)
Wold Primary School, Hull

My Monster Poem

My monster's name is Sully
My monster's favourite food is blood sweets
He lives under Mrs Harker's bed
He leaves slime on the bed covers
He stomps around
My monster eats fish eyes
My monster hates grown-ups
He slurps and burps
He is evil
My monster eats people's clothes
He is 9,000 years old.

He brings mud in the house
My monster eats all of the flowers in Mrs Harker's garden
He is scared of bats
He goes to Wold Primary School, Hull
He can fly like thunder
My monster goes to Hull fair
He is multicoloured with purple spots
My monster stays up until 12pm

Natasha Taylor (7)
Wold Primary School, Hull

My Monster Poem

He is hairy and rude
He lives down the loo
He eats pigs
He is ugly and he's
Got a moustache
My monster drags himself along
His name is Splatter
He is blue and he loves to
drive old cars.

Ryan Stothard (7)
Wold Primary School, Hull

In My School There Is . . .

In my school there is . . .
A painting on the wall of faces.
In my school there is screaming
Shouting at playtime break.
In my school there is . . .
A clatter of people running down
The corridor.
In my school there is . . .
An echoed voice running through
The hall.
In my school there is . . .
A squelch of the cleaner cleaning up.
In my school there is . . .
A click of lights going on.
But in my school there is . . .
A silence everyone can find . . .

While we're doing work . . .

Abigail Hastings (8)
Wold Primary School, Hull

My Monster Poem

He eats fish and chips and chocolate too
He crawls like a slug
Eats like a pig.

Looks like an ugly elephant
He lives in the bath
He has one hundred and fifty-five eyeballs
He is very, very friendly
He's called Slobbery Frobber
He has green and blue stripes with a purple spot
In the middle of his stripes.
He hates Manchester United
He supports Hull City like me.

Eden Scott Brown (7)
Wold Primary School, Hull

My Monster Poem

My monster is green,
My monster has a beard,
He has poky chops,
He has a beard going all the way down his chin,
He is lazy and greedy.

My monster eats?
My monster eats bones,
My monster eats my homework,
He eats my next-door neighbours,
He eats my reading books,
He eats my pets
He ate me!

How does my monster move?
He slurps and slides,
He spins around and round
He slimes around the living room
He slurps on me!

Where does my monster live?
My monster lives in the wild,
He comes into my kitchen and eats everything in the fridge,
He sleeps in the freezer.

Stacy Peacham (7)
Wold Primary School, Hull

Kennings

A man eater
A boat ripper
A fish killer
A coral destroyer
A fast swimmer
A strong sniffer
A quick catcher
A deadly hunter.

Jamie King (10)
Wold Primary School, Hull

The Wizard's House

In the cellar is . . .
A book full of spells,
An old wand in the corner,
A really rusty knife,
An old big pointed hat,
And the only sound is,
A door handle blowing in the wind.

In the kitchen is . . .
A case full of magic cooking books,
A wand flying in the air,
A strange looking table,
A drop of blood dripping from the wall,
And the only sound is,
A magic potion bubbling.

In the bedroom is . . .
A strange pair of pyjamas
An unlucky wand,
A magic book of spells,
An old chair in the corner,
And the only sound is,
The squeaking of the wizard laying on the bed.

In the attic is . . .
An old book of spells which is out of date,
A chest full of ingredients,
A wizard's broom,
A window that never closes,
And the only sound is,
The breeze of the wind blowing through the window.

Calum Thompson (8)
Wold Primary School, Hull

A Dream Come True

My magical dream box is like a glittering crystal
My memories of my grandad when I'm in bed
I like it flying on a plane to Spain to talk to the Spanish people.
I like having dreams about splashing in the sea
Swimming in the ocean and swimming with the dolphins.
I like having dreams about going to the South Pole
To groom the polar bear
I like going to the North Pole to see the penguins
Having a dream about my grandad when he was alive
In this box it's full of nature, of a boiling hot deserted place.
I would like to be a millionaire
So I could buy a mansion and let my mum come and live with me.
It's like a flaming hot volcano burning in my heart.
It's like a gleaming glittery crystal glittering in a bright gleaming ocean.

Emma Haywood (9)
Wold Primary School, Hull

My Box Of Dreams

My box is a square box . . .
A square box that's green and red
A square box that's green and red with dreamland in.
I can hear swords swishing and bows twanging in
Lord Of The Rings.
I wish I could play for Manchester United and England.
I wonder if I would have all the Playstation 2 games in the world.
A good dream is what I will tell you next.
Of being rich and owning a mansion
Or eating yummy burgers and scrummy pizzas all day long
Or travelling the world
I wish I could fly a supersonic jet over Hull for a really brilliant view.
Or I dream of playing for Hull City and going to every game for them.

Luke Wilkinson (9)
Wold Primary School, Hull

The Vampire's House

In the cellar is . . .
Horrid broken fangs with blood all over them,
Body parts everywhere with teeth marks in the necks,
A desk with killing plans on it,
A book with black laws in it
And the only sound is,
Teeth chattering in the distance.

In the kitchen is . . .
A pan cooking green snot,
An oven baking children's arms,
A table made out of disgusting bones,
A pet spider crawling across the floor,
And the only sound is,
The pan bubbling with green snot in it.

In the bedroom is . . .
A four poster bed filled with worms,
A lamp powered by electric eels,
A wardrobe full of capes and suits,
A toolbox so he can operate on teachers
And the only sound is,
Worms wriggling in the bed.

In the bathroom is . . .
Bats in the bath soaking in spiders,
Beetles in the sink full of cold water
Cat hairs on the toilet
Snakes slithering across the tiled floor
And the only sound is,
The hissing of the snakes.

In the attic is . . .
A big red rocking chair,
A box of old children's toys,
A table broken into bits,
A smashed mirror and bats on top of it,
And the only sound is,
The ghosts rocking the rocking chair.

Jennifer Hewson (8)
Wold Primary School, Hull

The Fairy's House

In the cellar is . . .
A pair of humongous wings,
A dinted broken crown,
A quarter of a wand,
A lot of dust from the magic spell,
And the only sound is,
The twinkling of the star from the quarter of the wand.

In the kitchen is . . .
A sink with bubbling dust,
A pair of sparkling shoes shining in the moonlight
A shining coat with enormous stars,
A pair of dancing shoes,
And the only sound is,
The dancing shoes tapping.

In the bedroom is . . .
A sparkling glittering dress,
Two pairs of tatty shoes,
A broken worn-out bed,
A cover with dust sprinkled over it
And the only sound is,
The birds singing loudly.

In the bathroom is . . .
A toilet with half a wand in it,
A bath shining clean,
A sink with the smell of dust,
A photo with a wand on it,
And the only sound is,
The wind coming through the window.

In the attic is . . .
A glowing case,
In the case is a magic pillow and a mirror,
In the mirror is a book,
A book of spells and a new wand,
And the only sound is,
The creaking of the floorboards.

Amy Kemp (8)
Wold Primary School, Hull

The Vampire's House

In the cellar is . . .
big jars of blood and little jars
coffins with spiders on
buckets of slime and slush
people's eyeballs in bowls and buckets
And the only sound is,
scuttling of the spiders.

In the kitchen is . . .
blood boiling in pans,
people's fat on the sideboard,
creepy crawlies crawling around,
a jar full of chopped bones
And the only sound is,
the boiling of the pans.

In the bedroom is . . .
a bed with rotten wood
a black cape with holes in
drawers full of mice
a musty old rotten smell
And the only sound is,
the bedroom door creaking.

In the bathroom is . . .
a glass with fangs in
a window being smashed
the floor all dusty and rotting away
a tap left running
And the only sound is,
the tap dripping.

In the attic is . . .
an old chair with bite marks in
a skull rotting away
old jugs of blood that stink
an old cape half ripped in half
And the only sound is,
the chair squeaking.

Jessica Harris (8)
Wold Primary School, Hull

The Hobbit's House

In the cellar is . . .
great barrels of rum, wine and beer,
tins of humongous deer ready to be feasted,
winding tunnels going under ground,
old animal bones with chew marks on
and the only sound is,
the beer spilling into fine cups.

In the kitchen is . . .
drawers crammed with different utensils,
humongous cupboards filling the room,
sharp knives and forks on the oak table,
and a dark tunnel that leads into darkness.
and the only sound is,
the whisking of a spoon.

In the bedroom is . . .
a four poster bed that views a grand old balcony
on a little table in front of a window is an empty frame
there are thousands of photos on the wall
and a velvet carpet on the stone floor
and the only sound is,
the spraying of the perfume.

In the bathroom is . . .
a polished brass toilet
a plastic sink with clear running water
rolls of silky toilet rolls
perfume on a sacking shelf
and the only sound is,
the flush of a toilet.

In the attic is . . .
mirrors laid on the dusty wall
two throne sized chairs
a king size royal stick
a cape hung on a bedstead
and the only sound is,
the singing of a Venetian music box.

Wesley Foster (8)
Wold Primary School, Hull

The Angel's House

In the cellar is . . .
A beautiful pair of broken wings,
A fairy photo frame,
A box of silver talons,
And a gorgeous pet pixie,
And the only sound is a soft twinkle.

In the kitchen is . . .
A soft pan with fur around it,
A mug with tea in it,
And a smooth fridge,
A fluffy floor,
And the sound is passing planes.

In the bedroom is . . .
A pretty four poster bed,
A pair of lovely curtains,
A pair of silky wings,
A shiny cushion,
And the only sound is people talking.

In the bathroom is . . .
A bar of clean soap,
A bubbling bubble bath
A good-looking toilet,
And an attractive sink,
And the only sound is a soft song coming from downstairs.

In the attic is . . .
A broken wand,
A pair of golden shoes,
An old rocking chair as still as a dummy,
And a treasure box,
And the only sound is birds singing.

Victoria Marshall (8)
Wold Primary School, Hull

The Wizard's House

In the cellar is . . .
an old worn out wand,
a crumbling, dusty cloak,
an old pointed starry hat,
a useless torn spellbook
And the only sound is,
pages being turned over.

In the kitchen is . . .
a magical frying pan,
a fantasy fridge,
a tap that only squirts out mysterious magic,
a boiling hot roasting oven.
And the only sound is,
the roasting of the oven.

In the bedroom is . . .
a drawer of fresh clean capes,
a bedroom full of flying wands,
a stack of multicoloured potions
a spellbook beside the bed.
And the only sound is,
the potions splattering about.

In the attic is . . .
a treasure chest full of jewels,
a picture of his great grandpa,
a jar of bronze money,
a glowing crystal ball.
And the only sound is,
the money clattering about.

Tim Sainty (8)
Wold Primary School, Hull

The Vampire's House

In the cellar is . . .
a skeleton hanging by his head on a piece of string,
a box of blood and bones,
a cup of fresh skin and a plate of eyeballs
a mirror with no reflection
and the only sound is,
a humming noise.

In the kitchen is . . .
a big wall with slime dripping off it,
an old cape with mice on it,
an old sofa with someone rotting on it,
a spare pair of fangs dripping poison,
and the only sound is,
the dripping of the poison.

In the bedroom is . . .
a knife covered with human flesh,
a wardrobe filled with mouldy clothes,
a person dead on the bed,
an arm half eaten,
and the only sound is,
the mould dropping off the clothes.

In the attic is . . .
a bag of people screaming
a ghost that's had its head chopped off,
a corner full of dust,
a pile of broken bones,
and the only sound is . . .
people crying for help.

Naomi Mason (8)
Wold Primary School, Hull

The Vampire's House

In the cellar is . . .
coffins of all different shapes and sizes,
spiders scuttling across the creaking floor,
jars of children's eyes and men's liver,
a trunk full of dead rotting bats,
and the only sound is,
the wind whirling through gaps in the walls.

In the kitchen is . . .
jars of eyes from cows and horses,
a tank of slime and slush,
a bin overflowing with owl wings,
a disgusting smell hanging in the air
and the only sound is,
the dripping of blood coming out of a tap.

In the bedroom is . . .
a cape covered in fresh blood,
a jar with fangs in it,
a window smashed with a sledge hammer,
a hypnotising whistle for animals,
and the only sound is,
the creature sleeping after a hard night's killing.

In the bathroom is . . .
bottles of potion stood on the side,
the shower running with green water,
a cupboard full of mouldy towels,
a mask just sitting on a shelf
and the only sound is,
the whooshing of the toilet flushing.

In the attic is . . .
a sack of smelly old bones,
a cage of trapped fairies,
a cupboard full of cobwebs and human's clothes,
a chest full of stolen jewellery
and the only sound is,
the howling of the wolf outside.

Eve Morton (8)
Wold Primary School, Hull

The Mummy's House

In a cellar is . . .
Ancient pillars of hieroglyphics,
A case in a 7,000 year old sarcophagus
A humongous sack of gold and secret treasures,
A huge golden phoenix,
And the only sound is,
The breezes of the wind through the broken window.

In the kitchen is . . .
A bucket full of scarab beetles,
A tank of crocodiles,
A cobweb filled with locusts,
A transparent tank with two scorpions,
And the only sound is,
The scuttling of the scarabs.

In the bedroom is . . .
Two large golden guardians guiding the entrance,
A little tank filled with snakes and giant millipedes,
And the surface covered with dusty sand like a little desert,
And palm trees surround the case in the sandy place,
And the only sound is,
The slimy snakes slithering around.

In the bathroom is . . .
A sandy towel with spiders clung onto it,
A wrap with a patch of blood,
A tap dripping with green liquid,
A pyramid scale with a snake design,
And the only sound is,
The rain tapping on the window from outside.

In the attic is . . .
An old cracked sacrificing pot,
A sculpture of a gold scorpion,
A statue of Nefertiti,
The only sound is
The squeaking of the bats, which hang upside down.

Jack Walsh (8)
Wold Primary School, Hull

The Devil's House

In the cellar is . . .
a flaming torch burning innocent people
a broken bag of bones
a blood red jar of blood and flesh
a jar of eyeballs
and the only sound is,
the cracking noise of the torch.

In the kitchen is . . .
a bag of bones broken cracked on the murky bog floor
a jar of blood
an enormous case of skulls
a pan of people
and the only sound is,
people crying for help.

In the bedroom is . . .
a mirror that is cracked
a window letting no air in
a four poster bed falling to pieces
a bat flying
and the only sound is,
the bat flying.

Harry John Foster (8)
Wold Primary School, Hull

St Bernard

A messy bed
A tail wagger
A mess maker
A bone chewer
A stick catcher
A drool monster
A hyperactive
A loving dog.

Amy Twidale (10)
Wold Primary School, Hull

Hagrid's House

In the kitchen is . . .
An enormous old dusty stove
A pewter tankard filled with frothy butterbeer
A crumpled recipe book for potions
A logi knife for cutting Fang's red juicy meat
and the only sound is,
the bulky sizzling pan.

In the bedroom is . . .
A massive and spacious bed
his fur coat all smelly
his wooden table is rolled
his milk all sour and cold
and the only sound is,
the wind sizzling.

In the attic is . . .
An old spell book all dusty
A wizard's hat with a rat inside
a newspaper bitten
A net is broken, hanging on the wall
and the only sound is,
the squeak of the rat.

Jason Carey (8)
Wold Primary School, Hull

My Box

In my box there is a dream
And in that dream there is an island
On that island there is a cave
In that cave there is an ocean
In that ocean there are dolphins
Dolphins jumping and diving.

Emmie Foster (9)
Wold Primary School, Hull

The Bogeyman's House

In the cellar is . . .
A pot of children's eyeballs,
A jar of blood,
A pot of flesh,
A jar of liver,
And the only sound is,
Him laughing upstairs.

In the kitchen is . . .
A pot full of children ready to cook and eat,
A jar of venom on the shelf,
A pan full of tricks,
Ropes all over the place,
And the only sound is,
The children bubbling in the pot.

In the bedroom is . . .
A pot of bogeys lying on the black, cold, slippery floor,
A bed with old curtains hanging from the wood at the top,
There are old cloaks lying on the floor,
A knife covered in red blood,
And the only sound is,
The screaming of children.

In the attic is . . .
An enormous red case,
A glowing crystal ball,
An old dusty spell book,
A broken wizard's wand,
And the only sound is,
The creaking floorboards.

Chloé Hayzelden (8)
Wold Primary School, Hull

The Fairy's House

In the cellar is . . .
A tub of glowing dust,
A broken wand,
A mini pair of shoes,
A lot of shooting stars,
And the only sound is,
The twinkling of the stars shooting around the room.

In the kitchen is . . .
A spare pair of wings,
A tiny handbag full of dust,
A sink of bubbling water,
A spell book covered with bubbles,
And the only sound is,
The bubbling of the water.

In the bedroom is . . .
Six pink dresses,
Six pink and yellow shoes,
Three pairs of wings,
A shiny mirror bright and new,
And the only sound is,
The wind blowing through the window.

In the bathroom is . . .
A shower that only sprinkles dust,
A cupboard full of perfume fresh and clean,
Towels stacked up high,
A small radiator with a fresh smell of flowers
And the only sound is,
The sprinkling of the dust from the shower.

In the attic is . . .
A broken mirror without any glass,
A pixie's bed with spiders on it,
An old grey magic book,
An ancient red and gold chair,
And the only sound is,
The sound of the birds chirping on the roof.

Catherine Welham (8)
Wold Primary School, Hull

The Devil's House

In the cellar is . . .
a big jar of gooey flesh,
an enormous bottle of phlegm,
a gloomy chair that never stops rocking,
a window that has no air coming in.
And the only sound is,
the jars crashing on the floor.

In the kitchen is . . .
a humongous jar of eyeballs
a big bubbling cooker,
a pan full of bones
a groaning bag of skulls.
And the only sound is,
people crying for help.

In the bedroom is . . .
a massive bed it can just get into
an ancient picture on the wall
a skeleton hung on the wall
a person locked in a box
And the only sound is,
the slamming on the box.

In the attic is . . .
a mirror with no glass in it
a black and white cat that lives in the corner,
a haunted ghost that only comes out at night,
a table with only one leg.
And the only sound is,
the floor creaking.

Joe Morris (8)
Wold Primary School, Hull

My Grandad's House

My grandma and grandad
Have a picture of my dad
There in a shiny gold photo frame.
They used to have a coal fire
With a beautiful gold edging.
My grandad has some goldfish
(He sometimes puts them in the bath)
They also have a poodle dog.
My grandma and my brother Dan are on a photo.
My brother Dan won first prize.
My grandma has it proudly on her wall.
They have lovely things in their house.

Megan Hackford (9)
Wold Primary School, Hull

View Of A Meat Eater Cheetah

A meat eater
A fast mover
A prey hunter
A great fighter
A meat swallower
A man eater
A spotty prey.

Ricky Hookem (10)
Wold Primary School, Hull

Angry Tanka

I want to shout out
I want to scream out aloud
Because I am mad
Nothing has gone right today
I can't wait for tomorrow.

Jack Laverick (10)
Wold Primary School, Hull

Smarties

What does it sound like can you guess?
What does it look like?
What does it feel like?
What does it smell like?
What does it taste like?

It sounds like food being put in the frying pan without being put
on the food,
Sizzling very loud at sixty degrees.

It looks like a UFO flying round the galaxy whooshing around like
a car racing on racetracks.

It feels like a smooth sweet rolling across your hand very slowly
like a tortoise and like a moon rising in the sky.

A smelly melting chocolate very slowly and like melting ice being
poured out of the ice case and tomato sauce being poured
out of the bottle.

It tastes like hot chocolate melting in your mouth
rolling down the back of your throat very slowly
like a snail moving, giving taste to your tastebuds.

Gareth Hales (10)
Wold Primary School, Hull

My Best Animals

The owl is flying out like a hunter.
The rabbit is sitting down eating slowly and drinking
water like sitting at a table having tea with a three year old.
The cat is playing with a ball of wool making a mess
like my bedroom.
The dog sleeps on my bean bag like a very sleepy baby.
The donkey is in the farm eating apples like a pen writing
on a pad of paper.
All the animals fall asleep in the shed nice and warm.

Chelsea Shepherd (10)
Wold Primary School, Hull

Smarties

It sounds like rustling trees
It sounds like a sizzling BBQ
It sounds like a boy kicking stones
It sounds like a waterfall falling from the top of a cliff
It looks like Saturn in space
It looks like a blazing fireball shooting across the Earth
It looks like a snowflake softly dropping from the sky
It looks like a pretty angel
It sounds like the freedom
It smells like delightful chocolate
It smells like Turkish Delight
It smells like blossom growing on trees
It feels like a ruby
It feels like a sweet flower
It feels like a smooth sweety
It feels like a sandy beach
It tastes like a calm piece of chocolate
It tastes like caramel chocolate
It tastes like fresh air
It tastes like a precious ruby.

Adam Owston-Dale (10)
Wold Primary School, Hull

Box Of Dreams

My box of dreams is diamond shaped
I keep my precious dreams in it.
It is orange with yellow checks on with red ribbon.
It is like a hurricane dropping down on me.
It is like a sandy cave with stones in it.
It is like Hull FC at the top of the table.
It is like whizzing snow falling gently on cars.
I dreamed I would play for Man Utd with Richard Clayphan.

Joshua Rae (9)
Wold Primary School, Hull

In My House I Hear . . .

In my house I hear my mum ironing.
In my house I hear my dad working really hard.
It's a loud sound.
It is bang! Bang! Bang!
In my house you can hear the birds
tweeting through my bedroom window.
In my house you can hear my brother doing
his homework and scrapings from his pen.
In my house you can hear my brother on the
really! Really! Really! loud PlayStation 2.
In my house you can hear the washing machine
spinning round and round.
In my house you can hear drip, drop coming from the tap.

Ryan Gagg (8)
Wold Primary School, Hull

In My House There Is . . .

In my house there is a picture of me
That glitters on the wall.
A TV that shines and sparkles.
A nice blue plate that stands on a
Stand and glitters.
A pillow that is fluffy and soft.
A PlayStation 2 that is clean with no dust.
A window that's see through and shines.
A teddy bear that's soft, squishy, cuddly,
And makes me cosy.
A lamp that shines and makes a rainbow
On the wall with jewels.

Alexander Powell (9)
Wold Primary School, Hull